D0872016

DISCARD

ATLAS OF EXTINCTION

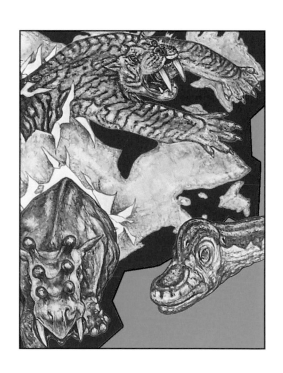

First published in 2002 by
Grolier Educational
Sherman Turnpike
Danbury, Connecticut 06816
© Quartz Editions 2002

All rights in this book are reserved. No part of this book may be used
or reproduced in any manner whatsoever or transmitted in any form or
by any means, electronic or mechanical, including photocopying,
recording, or any information storage and retrieval system, without
written permission of the copyright owner except in the case of brief
quotations embodied in critical articles and reviews. For information,
address the publishers:
Grolier Educational, Sherman Turnpike, Danbury, Connecticut 06816.

Library of Congress Cataloging-in-Publication Data
Extinct species.
        p. cm.
   Contents: v. 1. Why extinction occurs - - v. 2. Prehistoric animal life - - v. 3. Fossil
hunting - - v. 4. Extinct mammals - - v. 5. Extinct birds - - v. 6 Extinct underwater life - -
v. 7. Extinct reptiles and amphibians - - v. 8. Extinct invertebrates and plants - - v. 9.
Hominids - - v. 10. Atlas of extinction.
   Summary: Examines extinct species, including prehistoric man, and discusses why
extinction happens, as well as how information is gathered on species that existed
before humans evolved.
ISBN 0-7172-5564-6 (set) - - ISBN 0-7172-5565-4 (v. 1) - - ISBN 0-7172-5566-2 (v. 2)
- - ISBN 0-7172-5567-0 (v. 3) - - ISBN 0-7172-5568-9 (v. 4) - - ISBN 0-7172-5569-7 (v.
5) - - ISBN 0-7172-5570-0 (v. 6) - - ISBN 0-7172-5571-9 (v. 7) - - ISBN 0-7172-5572-7
(v. 8) - - ISBN 0-7172-5573-5 (v. 9) - - ISBN 0-7172-5574-3 (v. 10)
   1. Extinction (Biology) - - Juvenile literature. 2. Extinct animals - - Juvenile literature.
[1. Extinction (Biology) 2. Extinct animals.] I. Grolier Educational.

QH78 .E88 2002
578.68 - - dc21   2001055702

Produced by Quartz Editions
Premier House
112 Station Road
Edgware HA8 7BJ
UK

EDITORIAL DIRECTOR: Tamara Green
CREATIVE DIRECTOR: Marilyn Franks
PRINCIPAL ILLUSTRATOR: Neil Lloyd
CONTRIBUTING ILLUSTRATORS: Tony Gibbons, Helen Jones
EDITORIAL CONTRIBUTOR: Graham Coleman

Reprographics by Mullis Morgan, London
Printed in Belgium by Proost

ACKNOWLEDGMENTS

The publishers wish to thank the following for supplying
photographic images for this volume.

Front & back cover t SPL/J.Baum & D.Angus

Page 1t SPL/J.Baum & D.Angus;
p3t SPL/J.Baum & D.Angus;
p13tr SPL/J.Baum & D.Angus;
p15r SPL/J.Baum & D.Angus;
p17tr SPL/J.Baum & D.Angus;
p17bc NHPA/N.Wu; p19tr SPL/J.Baum & D.Angus;
p19tl NHM; p19br NHPA/M.Wendler;
p20tr NHPA/A.Rouse; p20bl NHPA/S.Krasemann;
p20br NHPA/H.Ausloos; p21tr, Antarctic, SPL/T.Van Sant,
Geosphere Project, Santa Monica;
p21tr, Arctic, SPL/J.Baum & D.Angus;
p21br NHPA/R.Planck; p22tc NHPA/D.Watts;
p23tr SPL/J.Baum & D.Angus; p23br NHM/M.Long;
p25tr SPL/J.Baum & D.Angus;
p27tr SPL/J.Baum & D.Angus; p28cr NHPA/D.Heuclin;
p29tr SPL/J.Baum & D.Angus;
p31tr SPL/J.Baum & D.Angus;
p31bl NHPA/N.Garbutt; p33tr SPL/J.Baum & D.Angus;
p33cl NHPA/G.Bernard; p33bl NHM;
p34bl NHPA/D.Heuclin; p35tr SPL/J.Baum & D.Angus;
p35c NHPA/G.I.Bernard; p37tr SPL/J.Baum & D.Angus;
p39tr SPL/J.Baum & D.Angus; p39tl NHPA/R.Tidman;
p40cl NHPA/K.Schafer; p41tr SPL/J.Baum & D.Angus;
p41br NHPA/D.Heuclin; p43tr SPL/J.Baum & D.Angus;
p45tr SPL/J.Baum & D.Angus

Abbreviations: Natural History Museum (NHM); Natural
History Photographic Agency (NHPA); Oxford Scientific Films
(OSF); Science Photo Library (SPL); bottom (b); center (c);
left (l); right (r); top (t).

EXTINCT SPECIES

ATLAS OF EXTINCTION

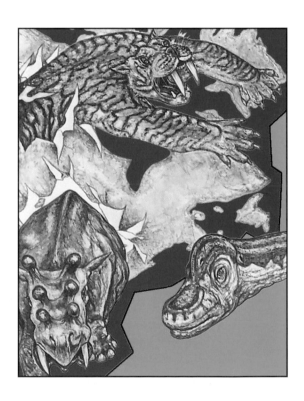

GROLIER EDUCATIONAL

SHERMAN TURNPIKE, DANBURY, CONNECTICUT 06816

LIBERTY LAKE
LIBRARY 99019

A PARROT'S PLIGHT
This is just one of several
parrots that have become
extinct in the West Indies,
as described on
pages 16-17.

RARE RABBIT
You would be hard-pressed to
find a specimen of this highly
endangered creature for the
reasons given on pages 14-15.

CONTENTS

PTEROSAUR TERRITORY
Where were remains of such winged reptiles first
discovered? And were they exclusive to that part of
the world? You can find out by turning to pages 44-45.

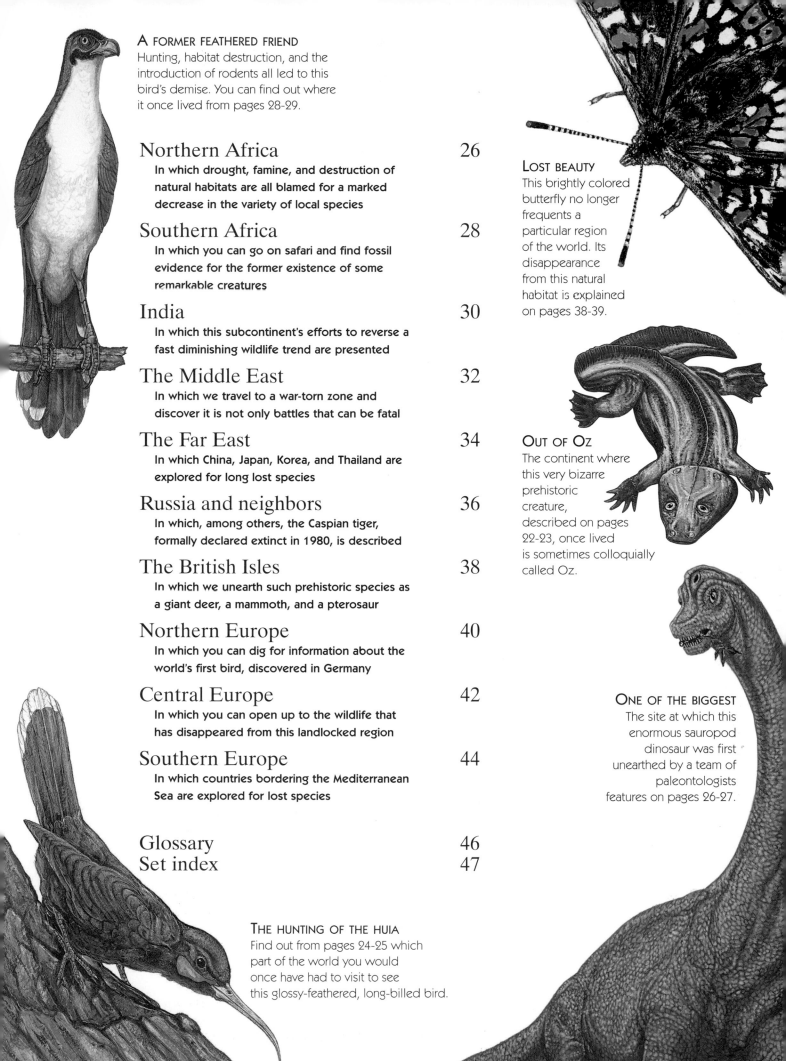

A FORMER FEATHERED FRIEND
Hunting, habitat destruction, and the introduction of rodents all led to this bird's demise. You can find out where it once lived from pages 28-29.

LOST BEAUTY
This brightly colored butterfly no longer frequents a particular region of the world. Its disappearance from this natural habitat is explained on pages 38-39.

OUT OF OZ
The continent where this very bizarre prehistoric creature, described on pages 22-23, once lived is sometimes colloquially called Oz.

ONE OF THE BIGGEST
The site at which this enormous sauropod dinosaur was first unearthed by a team of paleontologists features on pages 26-27.

THE HUNTING OF THE HUIA
Find out from pages 24-25 which part of the world you would once have had to visit to see this glossy-feathered, long-billed bird.

INTRODUCTION

The Arizona jaguar; the California coast grizzly; the Texas red wolf; the passenger pigeon; the heath hen; Carolina parakeets; and Badlands bighorn sheep – these are just some of the wonderful animals that have completely disappeared from the North American continent within the last 200 years, most of them needlessly.

But of course the United States is not alone in having lost a whole variety of wonderful species both long ago and recently. In fact, there cannot be a country in the world from which certain indigenous mammals, reptiles, marine life, insects, amphibians, and plants have not disappeared at one time or another.

THEN AND THERE
Remains of this Triassic plant-eating dinosaur have been found in places as far apart as South America and western Europe.

TO THE POINT
From its pointed teeth, ideally suited to tearing at flesh, scientists know this creature, dug up in Wyoming, was a carnivore.

FAR AND WIDE
Early humans probably hunted this creature, once found in parts of Great Britain. The antlers of the male spread far wider than its body.

BEFORE THE BIRDS
From fossils unearthed in Germany paleontologists have reached the conclusion that this extraordinary creature, which could only flutter but not fly, was an ancestor of today's birds.

Over the pages that follow we embark on a world tour, the aim of which is to discover which species have become extinct where. Did you know, for instance, that there may have been as many as 25 different types of moa, a flightless bird whose remains have only been found on the islands of New Zealand?

Use the index, too, to find out in which other volumes you can unearth more information about creatures that have vanished or are dying out in particular countries.

As you go from country to country while turning the pages of this book, you will also meet some of the severely endangered creatures that, for the moment, are still to be found in each region. It will then be for *you* to think about whether they are doomed or may perhaps be saved through prompt action.

PESTERED FOR ITS PELT
Human hunters are principally to blame for the demise of the sea mink. Its fur was once widely sought after, but nothing has been seen of it since the end of the 19th century.

HOW ODD!
The mysterious starling shown here certainly deserved its name. Only one dead specimen in poor condition was ever found.

GONE APE
The powerfully jawed creature shown *right* lived at the same time as some of our earliest ancestors and went extinct about 1 million years ago. Its remains have been found in various parts of eastern and southern Africa.

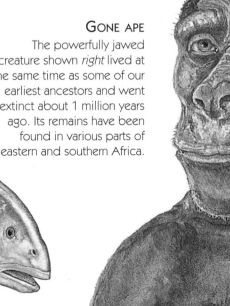

CAUGHT FOR SPORT
Not seen in streams and rivers since 1923, the New Zealand grayling, once regularly caught by anglers, is thought to have disappeared due partly to the introduction of other fish.

As the Continents Formed

Long ago the layout of all the world's land was very different from the way it looks today. South America and Africa, for instance, were once part of the same "supercontinent," and what is now the United States was joined to all of Europe.

According to modern scientific thinking, the position of land on Earth has been changing ever since our planet was formed 4.5 billion years ago or more. But most of these changes took place slowly over long periods of time and early on in the world's history. At first, all land was joined in one so-called "supercontinent" known as Pangaea (PAN-JEE-AH), meaning "all earth," which was completely surrounded by sea. Early creatures, such as the first dinosaurs, were free to wander the world. There were no ocean barriers to block their wanderings.

By the end of Triassic times, however – that is, 213 million years ago – Pangaea had started to break up into two main parts that scientists now refer to as Laurasia (LOR-AYS-EE-AH,) situated in the north, and Gondwana, in the south.

Eventually, by about 145 million years ago, as shown in the sequence of globes *below*, these two land masses started to subdivide further. What are now Africa and South America slowly separated, for example; India broke away, but North America and Europe were still joined as one area.

The continents then gradually moved even further apart. As this happened, the world also experienced changing weather conditions. Polar ice, for example, did not always exist at regions now known as the Arctic and Antarctic; and Earth has been subjected to drastically different climatic conditions at various points in the past, which have had enormous effect on the flora and fauna of this planet.

But what actually caused the breakup of Pangaea and its later further division into a number of separated land masses? Scientific study of the Earth's structure, the movement and layout of the land, and the formation (and disappearance) of oceans comes under the general heading of paleogeography.

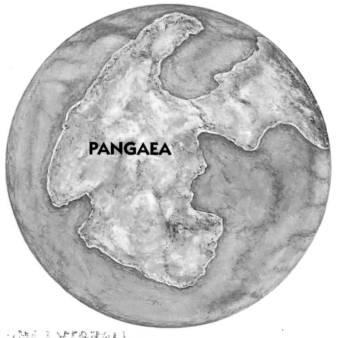

PANGAEA

LAURASIA

GONDWANA

ON THE MOVE

It was a scientist named Alfred Wegener who first suggested at the beginning of the last century that the continents must have moved their positions over time. However, it was not until the 1960s that paleogeographers first offered a full explanation. They found that on the floor of the oceans there is even now a network of enormous, very slow-moving plates that, driven by currents in the planet's mantle (the layer beneath its crust) and heat from deep within the Earth's core, carry the continents over the surface of the globe. This branch of paleogeography is known as plate tectonics.

Some seas have also vanished as vast areas of land changed position. Western North America, for example, is thought once to have been isolated by a stretch of water now given the name of the Great Interior Seaway.

In total, there are 8 large plates that move only about 1-2 inches each year in a process which scientists refer to as continental drift. The plates are normally rigid, but changes can occur at their edges. At a midocean ridge such as the one running down the center of the Atlantic Ocean, for example, the plates are moving apart. At other places, however, plates may approach each other. If they finally come so close that one will start to overlay the other, then mountains may form as a result of the collision. Indeed, this is how Asia's Himalayan range, the highest in the world, was originally created.

Earthquakes are also a sure indication of activity deep within the planet's core, causing part of the outer shell to move. In fact, hundreds of thousands of quakes occur every year, although most are so insignificant that they are not felt on the surface.

Fact file

● Geophysicists are scientists who study the structure of the planet's mantle and plates, and monitor any subtle changes.

● Earth measures about 24,902 miles around the equator (an imaginary line dividing the planet in half horizontally at its widest point.)

● It may seem strange that fossils of fish, marine reptiles, or seashells are sometimes found far inland and even in places as high as the Himalaya Mountains of Asia. But over huge expanses of time the Earth's surface and the oceans, too, have completely altered position. The land that now forms these mountains was once an ocean bed.

Sometimes, however, they open great cracks in the ground, as has occurred along the San Andreas fault in California.

LIBERTY LAKE LIBRARY 99019

9

THE WORLD TODAY

The world is, of course, round; but the maps further on in this book have jagged edges to show them as chunks cut out of a rolled out and flattened globe like the one *below*. What, then, are the main geographical features of each main region of our planet?

EUROPE
The continent of Europe lies entirely in the northern hemisphere – that is, above the imaginary line of the equator, which divides the world horizontally into two equal parts. Some areas consist of forest and woodland or mountains, grassland, heaths, and marshes; but farms and urban developments make up a huge proportion of this land mass. Among the many countries forming this continent are Belgium, England, France, Germany, Holland, Hungary, Italy, Portugal, Russia, Spain, and Switzerland.

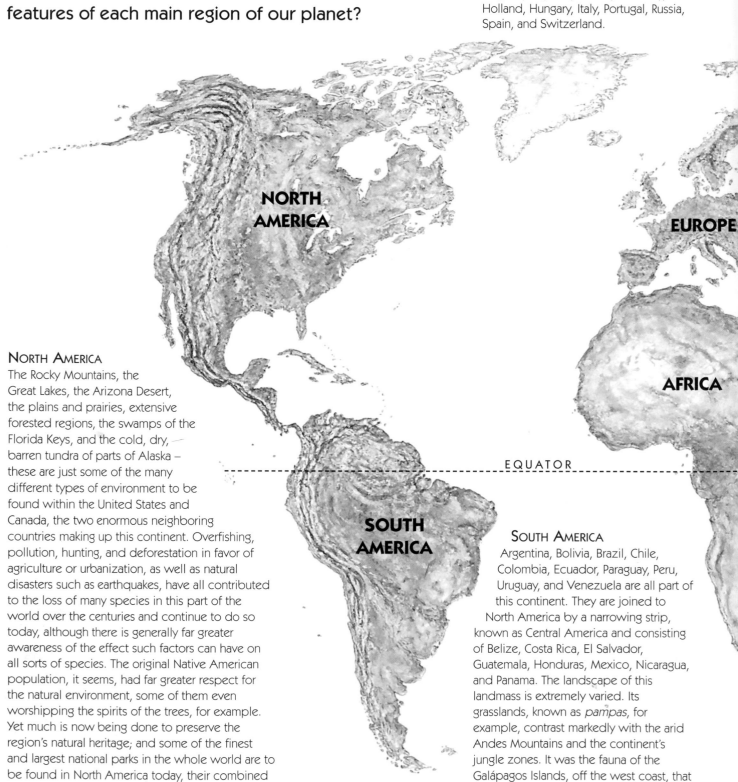

NORTH AMERICA

EUROPE

AFRICA

EQUATOR

SOUTH AMERICA

NORTH AMERICA
The Rocky Mountains, the Great Lakes, the Arizona Desert, the plains and prairies, extensive forested regions, the swamps of the Florida Keys, and the cold, dry, barren tundra of parts of Alaska – these are just some of the many different types of environment to be found within the United States and Canada, the two enormous neighboring countries making up this continent. Overfishing, pollution, hunting, and deforestation in favor of agriculture or urbanization, as well as natural disasters such as earthquakes, have all contributed to the loss of many species in this part of the world over the centuries and continue to do so today, although there is generally far greater awareness of the effect such factors can have on all sorts of species. The original Native American population, it seems, had far greater respect for the natural environment, some of them even worshipping the spirits of the trees, for example. Yet much is now being done to preserve the region's natural heritage; and some of the finest and largest national parks in the whole world are to be found in North America today, their combined range encompassing all the many types of geographical features of this continent.

SOUTH AMERICA
Argentina, Bolivia, Brazil, Chile, Colombia, Ecuador, Paraguay, Peru, Uruguay, and Venezuela are all part of this continent. They are joined to North America by a narrowing strip, known as Central America and consisting of Belize, Costa Rica, El Salvador, Guatemala, Honduras, Mexico, Nicaragua, and Panama. The landscape of this landmass is extremely varied. Its grasslands, known as *pampas*, for example, contrast markedly with the arid Andes Mountains and the continent's jungle zones. It was the fauna of the Galápagos Islands, off the west coast, that sparked the 19th-century British naturalist Charles Darwin's theory of evolution.

ASIA

Among the principal nations of Asia are Afghanistan, Bangladesh, Borneo, Brunei, Burma, Cambodia, China, India, Indonesia, Japan, North and South Korea, Laos, Malaysia, Pakistan, the Philippines, Taiwan, Thailand, Vietnam, and countries of the so-called Middle East, including Iran, Iraq, Israel, Jordan, Syria, Yemen, and others. Desert, semidesert, rain forests, woodlands, swamps, and grasslands can all be found across this vast continent. Rain-forest destruction has become a problem in Asia, and also fast disappearing are the mangrove forests, sometimes called the "forests of the sea" because they grow in areas that from time to time are flushed by salt or fresh water. Mangrove forests have ecosystems of their own; and destruction of this natural environment – many have now either been completely destroyed or stand at risk – has meant loss of their unique wildlife. But in some parts of Asia, such as Malaysia and Thailand, they are now managed under intensive conservation programs, and replanting is encouraged.

ASIA

Fact file

● According to one theory, there was once a lost continent known as Atlantis. It is said to have had a thriving culture but thought to have sunk beneath the ocean. No one knows exactly where it was sited, however, nor anything about its flora and fauna.

● Earthquakes and volcanoes show our planet is still in a state of change, so the position of many of the world's countries in an atlas of the distant future may be very different. Even now scientists can tell the Atlantic Ocean is getting very slightly wider every year, and Russia and North America are drifting a bit closer together. Entirely new continents may also form.

AUSTRALIA AND NEW ZEALAND

Situated in the southern hemisphere, Australia first became populated by settlers from Polynesian islands, whose direct descendants are now known as Aborigines. The native people of the two main islands that make New Zealand, meanwhile, are the Maoris. Not until the 18th century did European colonization begin in this region, following the arrival of the great British explorer Captain Cook. With them this wave of settlers brought many new plants and animals, some of which were to have a marked effect on the indigenous flora and fauna. Much of the central area of Australia consists of desert and semidesert; but there are forests and woodlands, too, though substantial areas have been taken for intensive farming.

AFRICA

The continent of Africa is where the human species is thought by some scientists first to have evolved, and it now comprises more than 50 different countries, among them Algeria, Ghana, the Ivory Coast, Kenya, Nigeria, Sierra Leone, South Africa, and Zimbabwe. There are jungles in some western parts of the landmass; but Africa also contains the world's largest desert, the Sahara. Drought and famine have occurred frequently in some impoverished areas over recent years, and local wars and uprisings have also hindered progress to a large extent. One of Africa's most interesting geological features, meanwhile, is its Great Rift Valley, a 6,000-mile-long crack in the Earth's crust. The most dramatic part is in the east, where the Rift Valley divides Kenya into two great sections. The rift first occurred about 20 million years ago, and it continues to get wider today.

AUSTRALIA

NEW ZEALAND

NORTH AMERICA

Across these two pages you will find illustrated just a few of the many creatures no longer to be found on the North American continent, most of them from way back in time. But there are also many species that have become highly endangered here far more recently.

The United States can rightly be proud to have established in the 19th century in Wyoming the world's first national park, Yellowstone. Since then very many more have been set up all over the North American continent. But, of course, such conservation measures can never provide a guarantee of the survival of a species.

KING OF THE BIRDS
Extinct since 1800, the painted vulture *right,* a heat-loving species, may have died out due to severe frosts. Formerly found in the state of Florida, this bird had a bald neck, cream plumage, a long bill, and a red crown. Centuries ago some Native American tribes decorated their pipes with its magnificent quills and called it the king of the birds.

ON A PLATE
Extinct since the end of Jurassic times and unearthed in western North America, *Stegosaurus* (STEG-OH-SOR-US) had a double row of upright plates along its back. Each of these plates is thought to have acted like a solar panel.

FOSSILIZED FLESH-EATER
From this skull found in Eocene rocks in Wyoming paleontologists can tell *Mesonyx* (MEES-ON-IKS), about the size of a small sheep, was a carnivore. It is the pointed teeth, ideal for tearing at flesh, that provide a clue. Its skull also shows many similarities to those of whales.

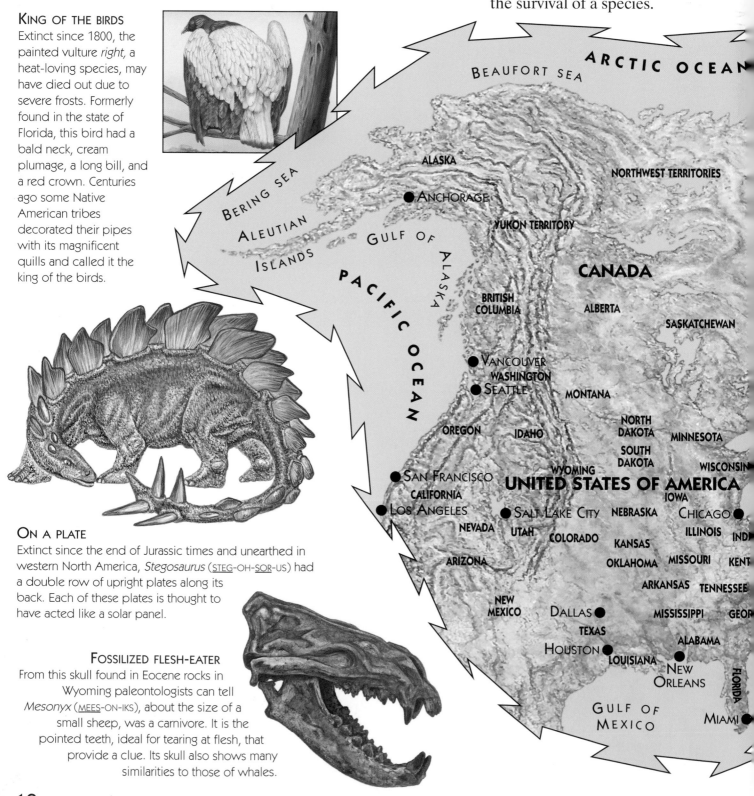

ARCTIC OCEAN
BEAUFORT SEA
BERING SEA
ALEUTIAN ISLANDS
PACIFIC OCEAN
GULF OF ALASKA
ALASKA
ANCHORAGE
YUKON TERRITORY
NORTHWEST TERRITORIES
CANADA
BRITISH COLUMBIA
ALBERTA
SASKATCHEWAN
VANCOUVER
WASHINGTON
SEATTLE
MONTANA
OREGON
IDAHO
NORTH DAKOTA
SOUTH DAKOTA
MINNESOTA
WISCONSIN
WYOMING
SAN FRANCISCO
UNITED STATES OF AMERICA
CALIFORNIA
IOWA
LOS ANGELES
SALT LAKE CITY
NEBRASKA
CHICAGO
NEVADA
UTAH
COLORADO
KANSAS
ILLINOIS
IND
ARIZONA
OKLAHOMA
MISSOURI
KENT
ARKANSAS
TENNESSEE
NEW MEXICO
DALLAS
MISSISSIPPI
GEOR
TEXAS
ALABAMA
HOUSTON
LOUISIANA
NEW ORLEANS
FLORIDA
GULF OF MEXICO
MIAMI

The cotton mouse of Florida; the Great Lakes sturgeon; the California condor; ridged rattlesnake of Arizona; the Cascade wolf of coastal British Columbia; and the Texas ocelot – these are just some of the continent's many endangered species.

In a reserve near you, too, there will be species in decline. Find out from the information service at such a park when you might stand the best chance of seeing such rare creatures, and if there is any way you can contribute to their well-being.

● One hundred years ago there were millions of prairie chickens in Texas. Today, however, there are precious few due to loss of habitat, drought, and predatory hawks and owls. Some are now being bred in captivity for release into the wild. But experience has shown that fewer than one in every fifty of the chicks survives for more than one year.

QUEEN ELIZABETH ISLANDS

VICTORIA ISLAND

BAFFIN ISLAND

HUDSON STRAIT

HUDSON BAY

MANITOBA

QUEBEC

LABRADOR

ONTARIO

NEWFOUNDLAND

MONTRÉAL

NEW BRUNSWICK

MAINE

NEW HAMPSHIRE

NOVA SCOTIA

VERMONT

MASS.

DETROIT

NEW YORK

CT. RI.

BOSTON

PENNSYLVANIA

NEW YORK CITY

PHILADELPHIA

MARYLAND

NEW JERSEY

WASHINGTON D.C.

DE.

NIA MD.

TH CAROLINA

TH CAROLINA

NORTH ATLANTIC OCEAN

UNDERGROUND HOME
Shaped like a corkscrew, this burrow of an extinct giant beaver descended to a depth of about 7 feet and dates from over 10,000 years ago. The first remains to be found of the 9-foot-long creature itself were dug up in Ohio in 1837.

GONE WILD
An ancestor of today's horses, *Mesohippus, below,* evolved on the prairies of North America. The central toe of its three-digited feet bore a hoof. Only later did horses spread to other parts of the globe. Wild horses no longer exist in North America, however, where they were once so successful.

AN EASY CATCH
The sea mink shown here once lived by the coasts of New England and the ocean off eastern Canada but was hunted by both Native American Indians and trappers for its skin and meat. The last survivor was killed in 1880. In general, hunters found it easier to catch than land-based mink.

CENTRAL AMERICA

Costa Rica, where the movie *Jurassic Park* was shot, was an ideal location because of its dense forests and natural wonders. It claims to live up to the meaning of its name, "rich coast"; but even that country's excellent conservation record is not without fault.

Central American squirrel monkeys are thought all to have retreated to a single reserve in Costa Rica because so much of their forest habitat has been thoughtlessly destroyed. But the situation elsewhere in this part of the world is considerably worse. Indeed, although much of its land is barren and desertlike, Mexico has unfortunately lost more than 90% of the forest habitat that did once form part of its landscape. Perhaps surprisingly, this has affected a visiting butterfly.

Each fall, for example, many millions of monarch butterflies instinctively migrate from North America.

Curiously, their destination is one particular Mexican forest 70 miles to the west of Mexico City, the capital. But the key to the survival of these delicate insects after an exhausting journey of over 3,000 miles is the quality of the forest where they must rest for the next six months before undertaking the return journey. Unfortunately, however, aerial photographs have shown that much of the forest has become patchy. As a result, the World Conservation Union has now declared restoration of this forest area of vital importance to survival of the monarch butterflies.

A CRY FOR HELP

There is only one small area of Mexico where the volcano rabbit, the only vocal member of its family, is found. It is a narrow strip, mostly open pine forest and coarse grasses, and only about 20 miles long and 10 miles across. Unfortunately, with every passing year this rabbit's natural habitat is decreasing due to the encroachment of agricultural land.

SHOT FOR SPECIMENS

A colorful woodpecker from the small island of Guadalupe off the Baja California coast, the flicker *above* is thought to have been killed in large numbers by goats and cats, and has not been seen since 1906, when collectors shot the last few pairs purely for the sake of stuffed specimens. There could not have been a more cruel or unnecessary end to this beautiful species.

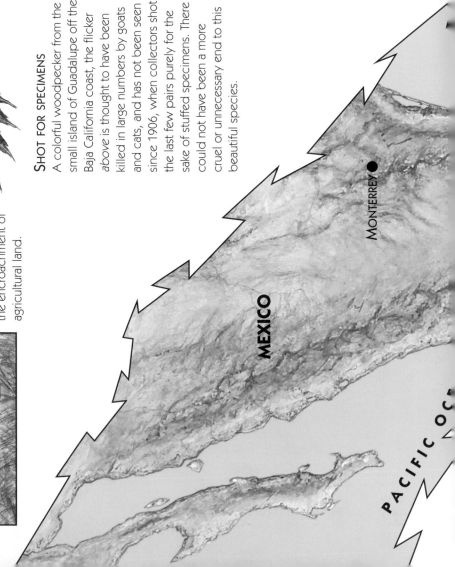

MEXICO

MONTERREY

PACIFIC OCE

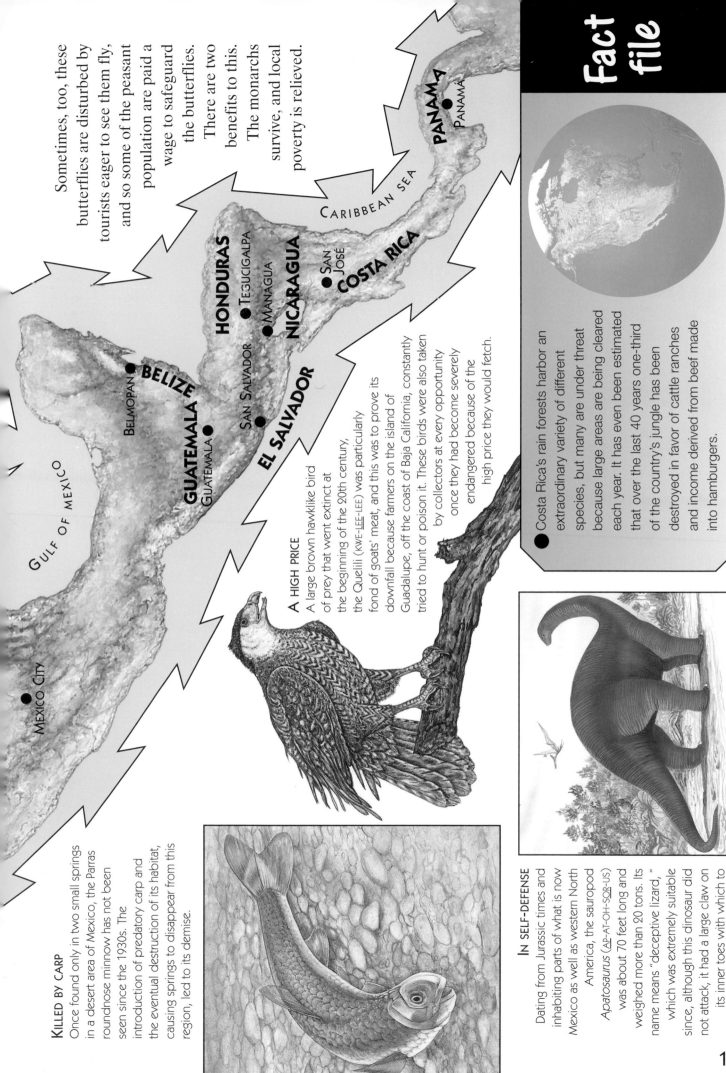

Sometimes, too, these butterflies are disturbed by tourists eager to see them fly, and so some of the peasant population are paid a wage to safeguard the butterflies.

There are two benefits to this. The monarchs survive, and local poverty is relieved.

- Costa Rica's rain forests harbor an extraordinary variety of different species, but many are under threat because large areas are being cleared each year. It has even been estimated that over the last 40 years one-third of the country's jungle has been destroyed in favor of cattle ranches and income derived from beef made into hamburgers.

PANAMA
Panamá

CARIBBEAN SEA

HONDURAS
Tegucigalpa
Managua
NICARAGUA

San José
COSTA RICA

BELIZE
Belmopan

GUATEMALA
Guatemala
San Salvador
EL SALVADOR

GULF OF MEXICO

Mexico City

A HIGH PRICE

A large brown hawklike bird of prey that went extinct at the beginning of the 20th century, the Quelili (KWE–LEE–LEE) was particularly fond of goats' meat, and this was to prove its downfall because farmers on the island of Guadalupe, off the coast of Baja California, constantly tried to hunt or poison it. These birds were also taken by collectors at every opportunity once they had become severely endangered because of the high price they would fetch.

KILLED BY CARP

Once found only in two small springs in a desert area of Mexico, the Parras roundnose minnow has not been seen since the 1930s. The introduction of predatory carp and the eventual destruction of its habitat, causing springs to disappear from this region, led to its demise.

IN SELF-DEFENSE

Dating from Jurassic times and inhabiting parts of what is now Mexico as well as western North America, the sauropod Apatosaurus (AP–AT–OH–SOR–US) was about 70 feet long and weighed more than 20 tons. Its name means "deceptive lizard," which was extremely suitable since, although this dinosaur did not attack, it had a large claw on its inner toes with which to defend itself from predators.

15

THE WEST INDIES

Throughout this part of the world it has been the widespread clearing of forested areas for the development of tourism and agriculture, introduced species that prey on native animals, and the taking of creatures for the pet trade that have led to the loss of much endemic wildlife.

Urban expansion particularly threatens the forests of Haiti and the Dominican Republic, which once together formed the island known as Hispaniola. But timber is also needed for firewood for cooking because, only too frequently, the island suffers from electricity blackouts that last for hours on end. Meanwhile, forest-dwellers, such as some types of cuckoo, have become increasingly rare, in one instance because the species is believed to have properties that ease the pain of arthritis and other conditions. A native iguana that can grow up to 3 feet in length is fast disappearing, too. Topsoil washed into the sea is also slowly choking local reefs.

DISHED UP IN THE DOMINICAN REPUBLIC
Known locally as house rats, hutias from the island of Hispaniola (now divided into Haiti and the Dominican Republic) went extinct in the mid-19th century. These rabbit-sized creatures were slow breeders, which probably contributed to their demise; but although rodents, they were also regularly hunted for their flesh.

If we are to save the flora and fauna, some of it exclusive to Haiti and found in its nine different biomes, ranging from cloud-forested, mountainous zones to fertile river valleys, conservationists working at national parks that are struggling to survive will have their work cut out.

ATLANTIC OCEAN

BAHAMAS

HAVANA

CUBA

CARIBBEAN SEA

SANTIAGO DE CUBA

HAI

PORT-AU-PRIN

JAMAICA

KINGSTON

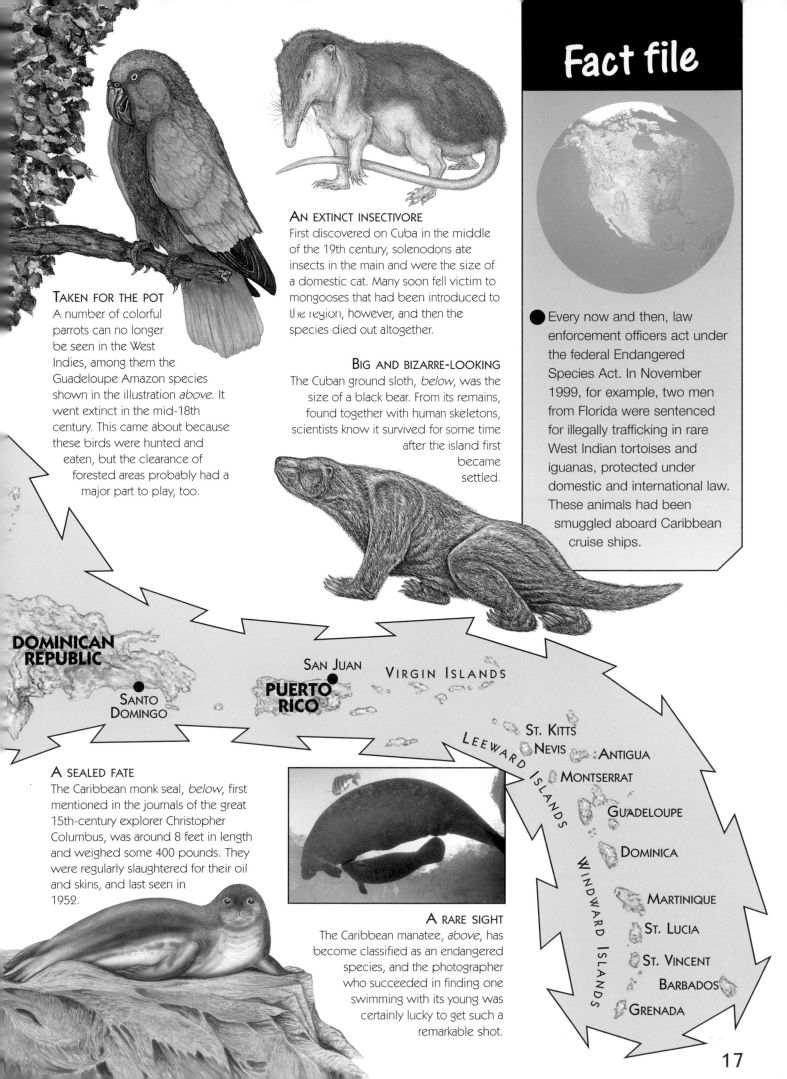

TAKEN FOR THE POT
A number of colorful parrots can no longer be seen in the West Indies, among them the Guadeloupe Amazon species shown in the illustration *above*. It went extinct in the mid-18th century. This came about because these birds were hunted and eaten, but the clearance of forested areas probably had a major part to play, too.

AN EXTINCT INSECTIVORE
First discovered on Cuba in the middle of the 19th century, solenodons ate insects in the main and were the size of a domestic cat. Many soon fell victim to mongooses that had been introduced to the region, however, and then the species died out altogether.

BIG AND BIZARRE-LOOKING
The Cuban ground sloth, *below*, was the size of a black bear. From its remains, found together with human skeletons, scientists know it survived for some time after the island first became settled.

Fact file

● Every now and then, law enforcement officers act under the federal Endangered Species Act. In November 1999, for example, two men from Florida were sentenced for illegally trafficking in rare West Indian tortoises and iguanas, protected under domestic and international law. These animals had been smuggled aboard Caribbean cruise ships.

DOMINICAN REPUBLIC

SANTO DOMINGO

SAN JUAN

PUERTO RICO

VIRGIN ISLANDS

ST. KITTS
NEVIS
ANTIGUA
LEEWARD ISLANDS
MONTSERRAT
GUADELOUPE
DOMINICA
WINDWARD ISLANDS
MARTINIQUE
ST. LUCIA
ST. VINCENT
BARBADOS
GRENADA

A SEALED FATE
The Caribbean monk seal, *below*, first mentioned in the journals of the great 15th-century explorer Christopher Columbus, was around 8 feet in length and weighed some 400 pounds. They were regularly slaughtered for their oil and skins, and last seen in 1952.

A RARE SIGHT
The Caribbean manatee, *above*, has become classified as an endangered species, and the photographer who succeeded in finding one swimming with its young was certainly lucky to get such a remarkable shot.

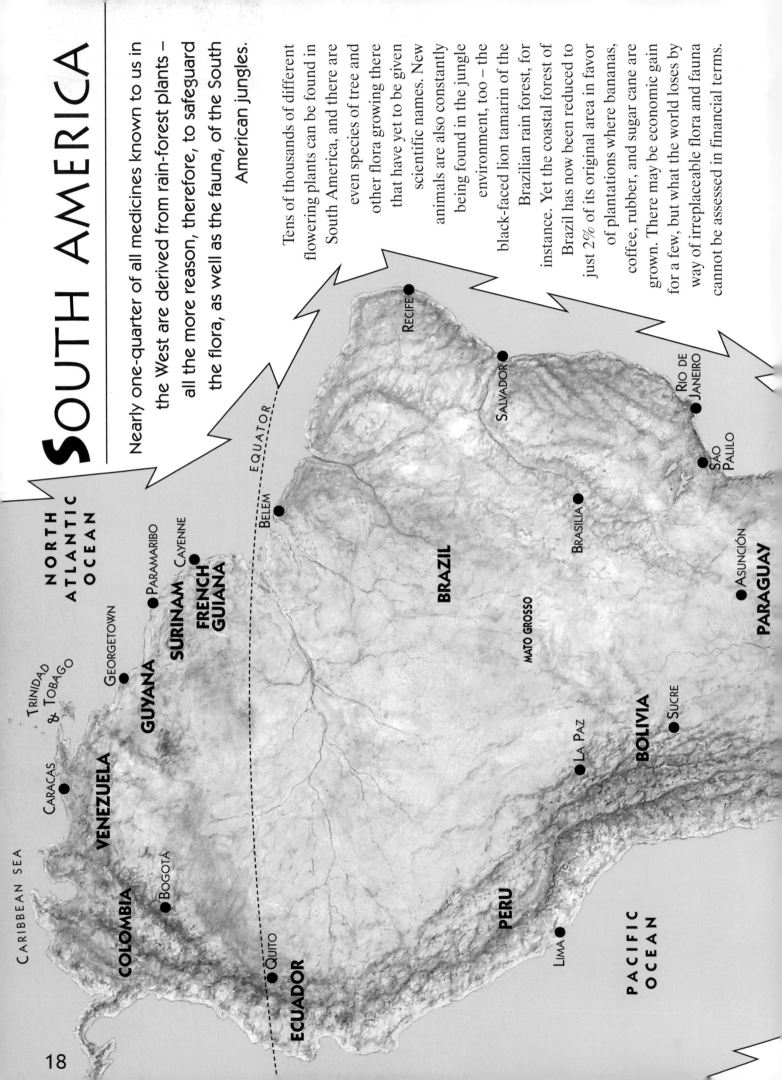

SOUTH AMERICA

Nearly one-quarter of all medicines known to us in the West are derived from rain-forest plants – all the more reason, therefore, to safeguard the flora, as well as the fauna, of the South American jungles.

Tens of thousands of different flowering plants can be found in South America, and there are even species of tree and other flora growing there that have yet to be given scientific names. New animals are also constantly being found in the jungle environment, too – the black-faced lion tamarin of the Brazilian rain forest, for instance. Yet the coastal forest of Brazil has now been reduced to just 2% of its original area in favor of plantations where bananas, coffee, rubber, and sugar cane are grown. There may be economic gain for a few, but what the world loses by way of irreplaceable flora and fauna cannot be assessed in financial terms.

CARIBBEAN SEA

NORTH ATLANTIC OCEAN

EQUATOR

PACIFIC OCEAN

TRINIDAD & TOBAGO

VENEZUELA

CARACAS

COLOMBIA

BOGOTÁ

GUYANA

GEORGETOWN

SURINAM

PARAMARIBO

FRENCH GUIANA

CAYENNE

ECUADOR

QUITO

BELEM

PERU

LIMA

BRAZIL

MATO GROSSO

RECIFE

SALVADOR

BRASILIA

RIO DE JANEIRO

SÃO PALILO

BOLIVIA

LA PAZ

SUCRE

PARAGUAY

ASUNCIÓN

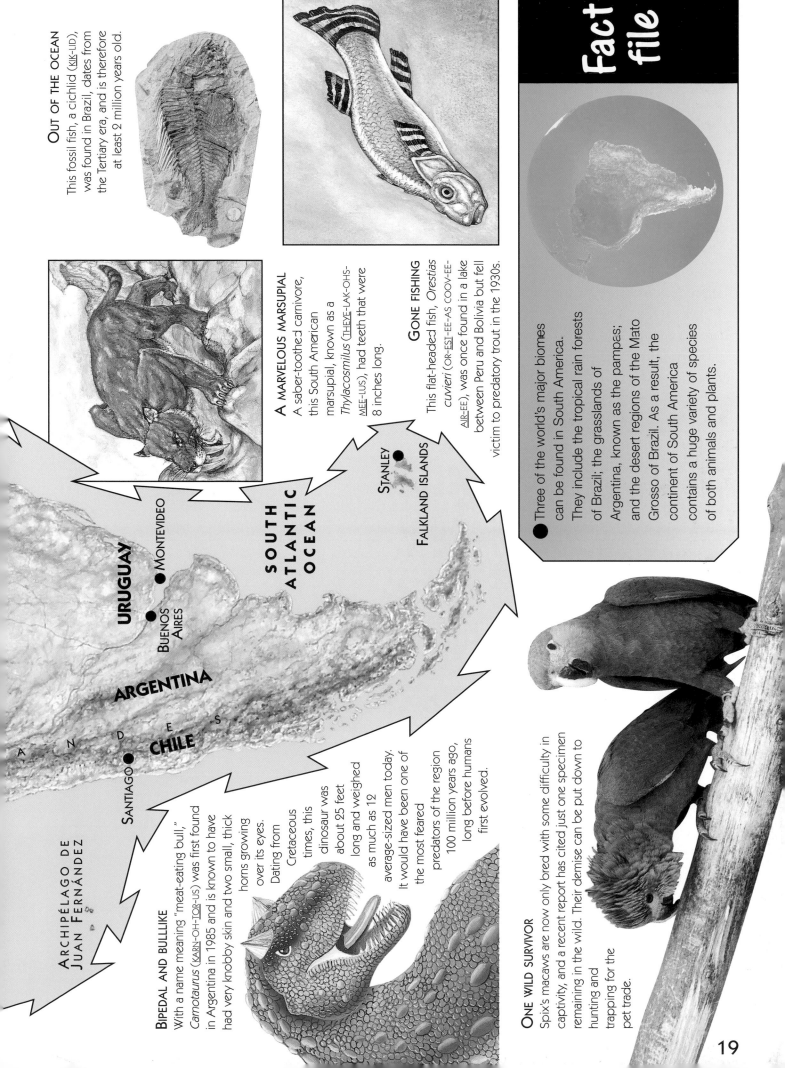

Out of the ocean

This fossil fish, a cichlid (KIK-lid), was found in Brazil, dates from the Tertiary era, and is therefore at least 2 million years old.

A marvelous marsupial

A saber-toothed carnivore, this South American marsupial, known as a *Thylacosmilus* (THEYE-LAK-OHS-MEE-lus), had teeth that were 8 inches long.

Gone fishing

This flat-headed fish, *Orestias cuvieri* (OR-EST-EE-AS COOV-EE-AIR-EE), was once found in a lake between Peru and Bolivia but fell victim to predatory trout in the 1930s.

Fact file

- Three of the world's major biomes can be found in South America. They include the tropical rain forests of Brazil; the grasslands of Argentina, known as the pampas; and the desert regions of the Mato Grosso of Brazil. As a result, the continent of South America contains a huge variety of species of both animals and plants.

URUGUAY
●MONTEVIDEO

BUENOS AIRES●

STANLEY ●
FALKLAND ISLANDS

SOUTH ATLANTIC OCEAN

ARGENTINA

A N D E S

CHILE

SANTIAGO●

ARCHIPIÉLAGO DE JUAN FERNÁNDEZ

Bipedal and bulllike

With a name meaning "meat-eating bull," *Carnotaurus* (KARN-OH-TOR-us) was first found in Argentina in 1985 and is known to have had very knobby skin and two small, thick horns growing over its eyes. Dating from Cretaceous times, this dinosaur was about 25 feet long and weighed as much as 12 average-sized men today. It would have been one of the most feared predators of the region 100 million years ago, long before humans first evolved.

One wild survivor

Spix's macaws are now only bred with some difficulty in captivity, and a recent report has cited just one specimen remaining in the wild. Their demise can be put down to hunting and trapping for the pet trade.

POLAR REGIONS

At what are generally thought of as the top and bottom of the world lie two vast, seemingly barren areas – the Arctic and Antarctic. But they also harbor wildlife and have ecosystems that are vulnerable to even the slightest alteration.

In June 2001 the United Nations Environment Program announced that at the present rate gas and oil exploration may start to involve up to 80% of the Arctic, seriously threatening much of the area's wildlife, including polar bears and reindeer. Some of the region is protected, but other parts, particularly toward the south, are not. Meanwhile, global warming continues; and if it, too, goes on at the present rate, the Arctic Ocean could be completely free of summer ice by the end of this century. Monitoring stations are keeping careful records.

BEAR ESSENTIALS
Conservationists agree that to stop the polar bear population decreasing even further, we will have to exercise control over pollution, melting of the ice caps, and hunting in Arctic regions.

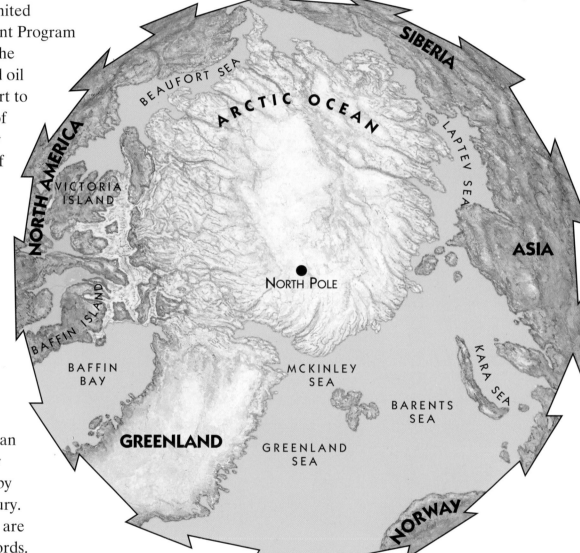

SIBERIA

BEAUFORT SEA

ARCTIC OCEAN

LAPTEV SEA

NORTH AMERICA

VICTORIA ISLAND

ASIA

NORTH POLE

BAFFIN ISLAND

KARA SEA

BAFFIN BAY

MCKINLEY SEA

BARENTS SEA

GREENLAND

GREENLAND SEA

NORWAY

THE DYING CARIBOU
The Peary caribou population has declined by a dramatic 95% over recent years, and there may now be only round 1,000 of these animals remaining in Arctic regions due to climate change.

SAVE THE ARCTIC FOX!
The Arctic fox, *right,* dark for part of the year but white during colder months, is now in decline. Cruelly hunted for its fur, it has also suffered from the expanded habitat of the red fox, its main rival; lack of food; and disease.

Scientists are also concerned that a huge hole in the protective ozone layer over Antarctica, one of the last true wildernesses on our planet, seems to have broadened even further, due partly to our use of gases known as CFCs. Indeed, this yawning gap in the stratosphere is said to have extended to the size of the entire continent of North America; and, of course, it may still be growing.

This hole does fluctuate in size, however. So optimists speculate that greater awareness of the terrible effects of pollution may well be successful in reducing the hole, though no one is sure how long it might take.

OUT OF THE BLUE
Found in both the northern and the southern hemisphere, blue whales like the one below, though endangered, are still killed for both their oil, derived from their blubber, and their meat.

FROM A WARMER ERA
This sauropod, aptly named *Antarctosaurus* (<u>ANT</u>-ARK-TOH-<u>SOR</u>-us), was unearthed from what many millions of years ago was once a tropical region.

Fact file

ANTARCTIC

ARCTIC

● Officially, all commercial whaling has been banned for many years in Antarctica, but it still continues illegally.

● If oil and minerals existing in the polar regions are ever fully exploited, conservationists fear it may wreak havoc among the wildlife of these parts of the planet. The effects of spillages, meanwhile, would be disastrous, possibly causing irreversible damage.

BY ACCIDENT
This black-browed albatross is resting on a rock shelf in Antarctica. Satellite tracking shows these beautiful birds, smallest of all albatrosses, are dwindling in number due to egg collecting and accidental deaths when diving for baited fishing lines.

WEDDELL SEA

SOUTHERN OCEAN

ANTARCTIC PENINSULA

BELLINGSHAUSEN SEA

AMUNDSEN SEA

ANTARCTICA

● SOUTH POLE

ROSS ICE SHELF

PACIFIC OCEAN

AUSTRALIA

The wondrous coral of this continent's Great Barrier Reef has been in decline for several years, and a number of endemic Australian species are dwindling, too. But every now and then something happens to make things look more positive.

Dry, flat, and featureless is how, in the past, one writer described the region of Lake Eyre in South Australia, 500 miles north of Adelaide, with its barren salt flats stretching far into the horizon. But in 2000, for only the fourth time in two hundred years, all that changed with the coming of monsoon rains. As if by magic, the scene was transformed, and a new inland sea, complete with its own tidal system, even though sited in the middle of a desert, now covered around 5,000 square miles.

Countless fish and birds, as well as insects and plants, many of them not seen in the region for a great many years and so thought to be locally extinct, soon returned once the salt deposits had dissolved.

Indeed, the rains were so heavy in 2000 that even at distant Ayers Rock, the most arid place on that continent as a rule, water gushed into waterfalls. But the new flourishing of life is unlikely to last, and no one knows when the next torrential rains will come. Could there be any better example of how survival of the world's flora and fauna is sometimes entirely at the mercy of the elements?

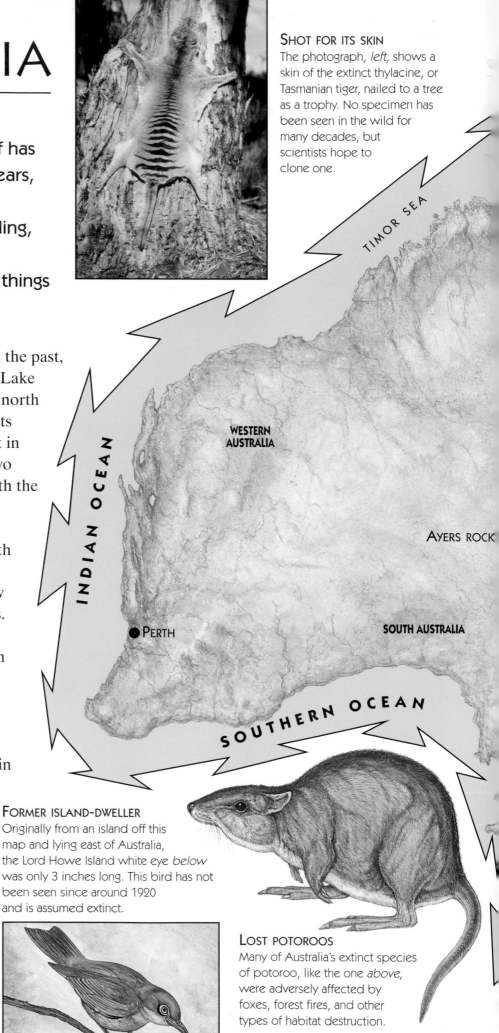

SHOT FOR ITS SKIN
The photograph, *left,* shows a skin of the extinct thylacine, or Tasmanian tiger, nailed to a tree as a trophy. No specimen has been seen in the wild for many decades, but scientists hope to clone one.

TIMOR SEA

INDIAN OCEAN

WESTERN AUSTRALIA

AYERS ROCK

● PERTH

SOUTH AUSTRALIA

SOUTHERN OCEAN

FORMER ISLAND-DWELLER
Originally from an island off this map and lying east of Australia, the Lord Howe Island white eye *below* was only 3 inches long. This bird has not been seen since around 1920 and is assumed extinct.

LOST POTOROOS
Many of Australia's extinct species of potoroo, like the one *above,* were adversely affected by foxes, forest fires, and other types of habitat destruction.

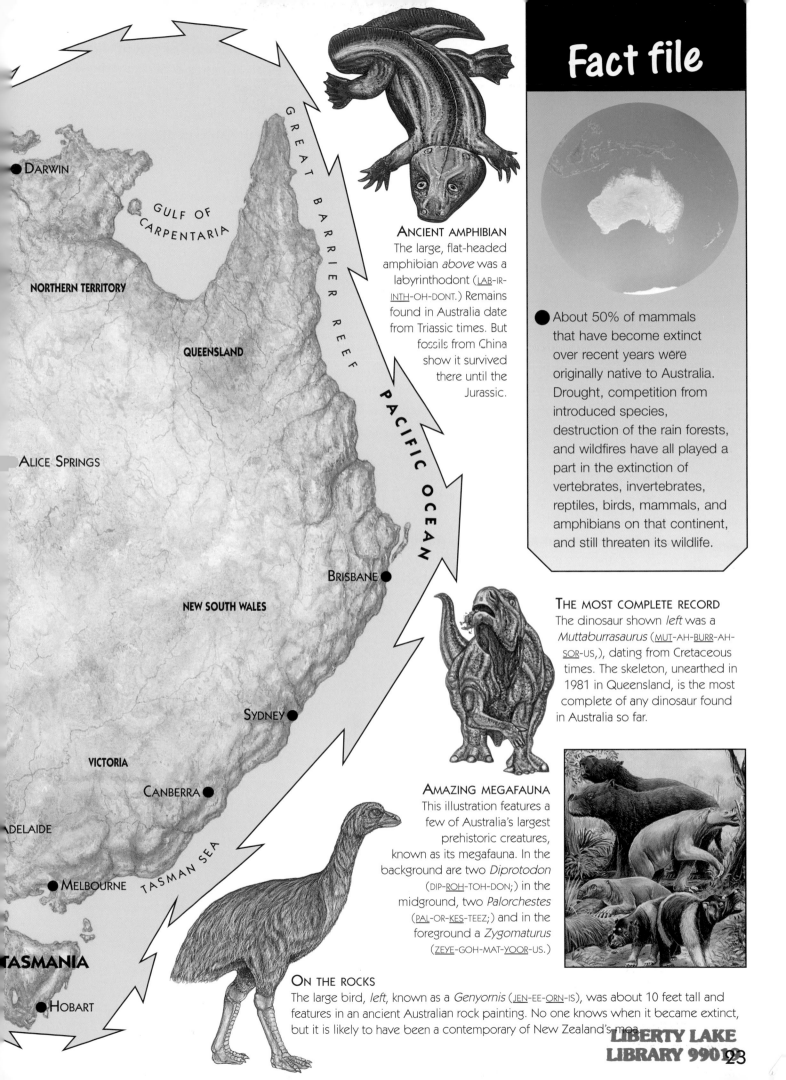

DARWIN

GULF OF
CARPENTARIA

NORTHERN TERRITORY

QUEENSLAND

ALICE SPRINGS

GREAT BARRIER REEF

PACIFIC OCEAN

BRISBANE

NEW SOUTH WALES

SYDNEY

VICTORIA

CANBERRA

ADELAIDE

TASMAN SEA

MELBOURNE

TASMANIA

HOBART

Fact file

● About 50% of mammals that have become extinct over recent years were originally native to Australia. Drought, competition from introduced species, destruction of the rain forests, and wildfires have all played a part in the extinction of vertebrates, invertebrates, reptiles, birds, mammals, and amphibians on that continent, and still threaten its wildlife.

ANCIENT AMPHIBIAN
The large, flat-headed amphibian *above* was a labyrinthodont (LAB-IR-INTH-OH-DONT.) Remains found in Australia date from Triassic times. But fossils from China show it survived there until the Jurassic.

THE MOST COMPLETE RECORD
The dinosaur shown *left* was a *Muttaburrasaurus* (MUT-AH-BURR-AH-SOR-US,), dating from Cretaceous times. The skeleton, unearthed in 1981 in Queensland, is the most complete of any dinosaur found in Australia so far.

AMAZING MEGAFAUNA
This illustration features a few of Australia's largest prehistoric creatures, known as its megafauna. In the background are two *Diprotodon* (DIP-ROH-TOH-DON;) in the midground, two *Palorchestes* (PAL-OR-KES-TEEZ;) and in the foreground a *Zygomaturus* (ZEYE-GOH-MAT-YOOR-US.)

ON THE ROCKS
The large bird, *left*, known as a *Genyornis* (JEN-EE-ORN-IS), was about 10 feet tall and features in an ancient Australian rock painting. No one knows when it became extinct, but it is likely to have been a contemporary of New Zealand's moa.

LIBERTY LAKE
LIBRARY 99019

23

NEW ZEALAND

Much of the wildlife found on the islands making up this archipelago are endemic to the region – that is, they are found nowhere else in the world. The careful management of native species in protected areas and national parks is therefore vitally important.

The fauna of New Zealand is unique in many ways. There are no snakes, for example, that exist only on this territory; and apart from a few types of bats and marine mammals, there are no land mammals exclusive to the islands either. But which species are now in danger and why?

New Zealand's Department of Conservation is responsible for all its native wildlife and works to ensure habitat protection, the control of predators, and the moving of species to a safer environment, if necessary. Another important aspect of this work is to assess the extent to which numbers are dwindling.

Currently, there are about 100 different species classed as Category A, which means they are most highly imperiled. The spiral sun orchid and the flightless kiwi are among them. Over 200 different species come under Category B.

But much is being done to promote their survival. Kiwi eggs, for example, are the subject of a recovery plan. Their eggs are removed from ground-level nests in some areas, so they are not at risk of being taken by predators. When the birds have hatched, they are raised to a size at which they can protect themselves more effectively and then released.

MORE ABOUT THE MOAS
When the Maoris came to New Zealand from Polynesia in the 10th century, they found as many as 25 different types of giant flightless birds that they called moas. Some were huge – more than three times your height – and all had evolved over millions of years. However, as soon as humans arrived, they began to hunt them for their flesh; and by the end of the 19th century all species of the family to which the moas belonged had gone extinct.

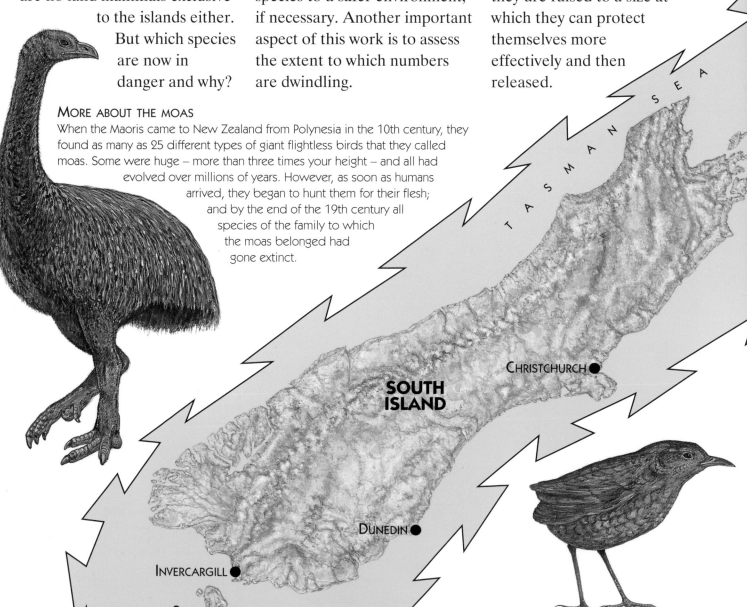

TASMAN SEA

CHRISTCHURCH ●

SOUTH ISLAND

DUNEDIN ●

INVERCARGILL ●

STEWART ISLAND

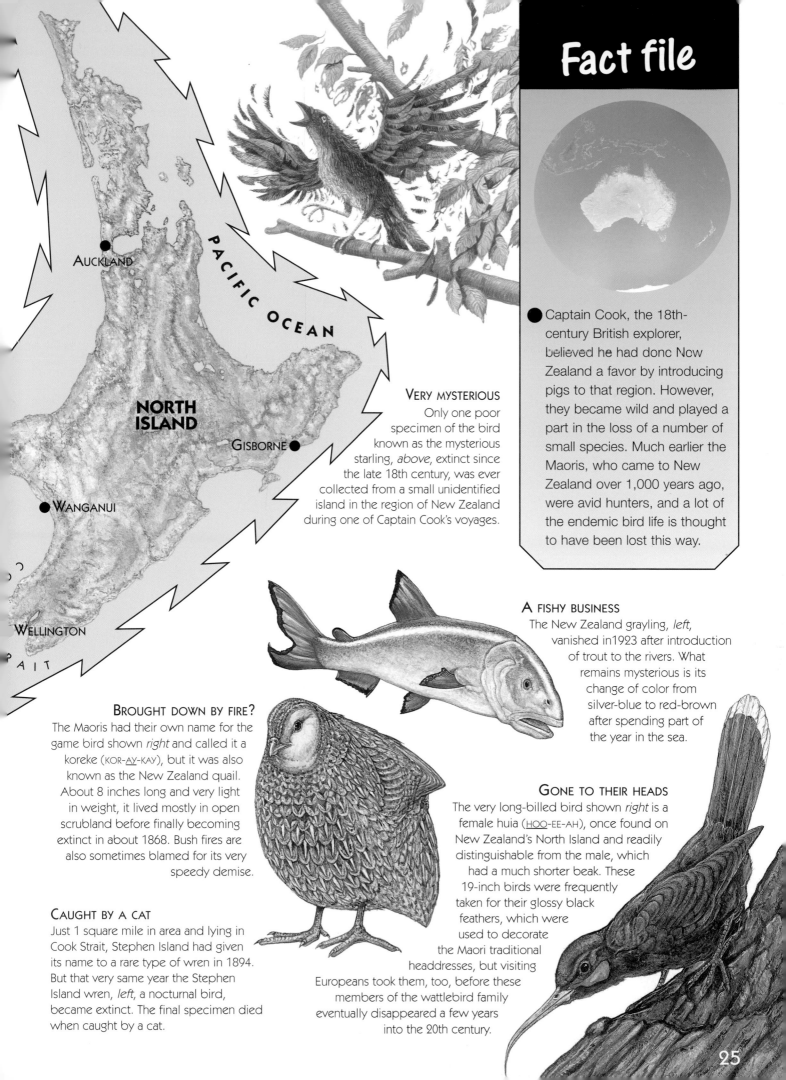

Captain Cook, the 18th-century British explorer, believed he had done New Zealand a favor by introducing pigs to that region. However, they became wild and played a part in the loss of a number of small species. Much earlier the Maoris, who came to New Zealand over 1,000 years ago, were avid hunters, and a lot of the endemic bird life is thought to have been lost this way.

VERY MYSTERIOUS

Only one poor specimen of the bird known as the mysterious starling, *above*, extinct since the late 18th century, was ever collected from a small unidentified island in the region of New Zealand during one of Captain Cook's voyages.

A FISHY BUSINESS

The New Zealand grayling, *left*, vanished in 1923 after introduction of trout to the rivers. What remains mysterious is its change of color from silver-blue to red-brown after spending part of the year in the sea.

BROUGHT DOWN BY FIRE?

The Maoris had their own name for the game bird shown *right* and called it a koreke (KOR-<u>AY</u>-KAY), but it was also known as the New Zealand quail. About 8 inches long and very light in weight, it lived mostly in open scrubland before finally becoming extinct in about 1868. Bush fires are also sometimes blamed for its very speedy demise.

GONE TO THEIR HEADS

The very long-billed bird shown *right* is a female huia (<u>HOO</u>-EE-AH), once found on New Zealand's North Island and readily distinguishable from the male, which had a much shorter beak. These 19-inch birds were frequently taken for their glossy black feathers, which were used to decorate the Maori traditional headdresses, but visiting Europeans took them, too, before these members of the wattlebird family eventually disappeared a few years into the 20th century.

CAUGHT BY A CAT

Just 1 square mile in area and lying in Cook Strait, Stephen Island had given its name to a rare type of wren in 1894. But that very same year the Stephen Island wren, *left*, a nocturnal bird, became extinct. The final specimen died when caught by a cat.

25

NORTH AFRICA

Conservationists fear that the disappearance in 2000 of an African monkey, once easy to find because it was brightly colored and lived in groups of 20 or more, may herald the extinction of several other species endemic to northern regions of that continent.

For the first time in two centuries a primate has been declared extinct. It was known as Miss Waldron's red colobus, and its habitat was the forests of Ghana and the Ivory Coast. Deforestation and urbanization have been to blame, and the animal had been listed as endangered since 1988.

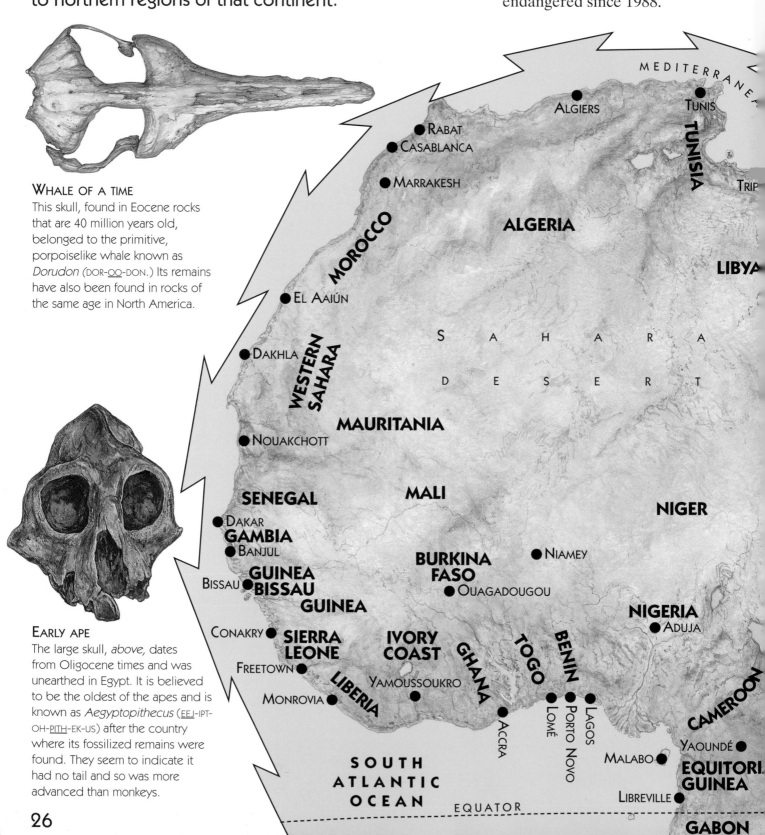

WHALE OF A TIME
This skull, found in Eocene rocks that are 40 million years old, belonged to the primitive, porpoiselike whale known as *Dorudon* (DOR-<u>OO</u>-DON.) Its remains have also been found in rocks of the same age in North America.

EARLY APE
The large skull, *above*, dates from Oligocene times and was unearthed in Egypt. It is believed to be the oldest of the apes and is known as *Aegyptopithecus* (<u>EEJ</u>-IPT-OH-<u>PITH</u>-EK-US) after the country where its fossilized remains were found. They seem to indicate it had no tail and so was more advanced than monkeys.

MEDITERRANEAN

ALGIERS

TUNIS

TUNISIA

TRIP

RABAT
CASABLANCA

MARRAKESH

ALGERIA

LIBYA

MOROCCO

EL AAIÚN

S A H A R A

DAKHLA

WESTERN SAHARA

D E S E R T

MAURITANIA

NOUAKCHOTT

MALI

NIGER

SENEGAL

DAKAR
GAMBIA
BANJUL

NIAMEY

BURKINA FASO
OUAGADOUGOU

GUINEA
BISSAU
BISSAU

NIGERIA
ADUJA

GUINEA

CONAKRY
SIERRA LEONE
FREETOWN

IVORY COAST
YAMOUSSOUKRO

GHANA

TOGO

BENIN

LAGOS
LOMÉ
PORTO NOVO

LIBERIA

MONROVIA

ACCRA

CAMEROON

YAOUNDÉ

MALABO

EQUITORIAL GUINEA

SOUTH ATLANTIC OCEAN

EQUATOR

LIBREVILLE

GABON

Much of the forest inhabited by the monkey had been fragmented by logging and the building of roads. Researchers trying to locate evidence of the survival of this creature, named after the companion of the collector who discovered it in 1933, have only found gun shells and other evidence of hunting. Local poachers are known to have shot or trapped them in considerable numbers for financial gain.

Indeed, one of the principal causes of decline in this region's wildlife has been the taking of animals for what is called the bush meat market. Other monkeys and larger mammals may soon be at serious risk in this region, too.

Fact file

- Long periods of severe drought leading to famine in Sudan, Chad, and other parts of northern Africa over recent years, as well as wars and internal strife in countries such as Sierra Leone and Algeria, may have heralded the extinction of a number of local species, among them possibly a few never scientifically identified. We will never know for sure.

TAKEN AS GAME
Extinct in Egypt and Tunisia, and hardly ever seen in Algeria and Libya, the addax, shown *right*, was once fairly widespread throughout the deserts of northern Africa but frequently taken by hunting parties.

AFRICAN GIANTS
Unearthed in Algeria, *Giraffatitan* (JIR-AF-AT-EYE-TAN), meaning "gigantic giraffe," was an 82-foot-long dinosaur from Jurassic times. It weighed in at 50 tons and was related to the dinosaur *Brachiosaurus* (BRAK-EE-OH-SOR-US), found elsewhere in Africa, Germany, and North America.

E A

● BENGHĀZI

ALEXANDRIA ●
CAIRO ●

LIBYAN DESERT

ARABIAN DESERT

EGYPT

RED SEA

● KHARTOUM

SUDAN

ASMERA ● **ERITREA**

DJIBOUTI
● DJIBOUTI

CHAD

● NDJAMENA

ADDIS ABABA ●
ETHIOPIA

CENTRAL AFRICAN REPUBLIC

BANGUI ●

SOMALIA

INDIAN OCEAN

MOGADISHU ●

SOUTHERN AFRICA

Madagascar, an island off the east coast of the southern part of the African continent, was once known as the naturalist's Promised Land because of the huge diversity of species to be found there. Now, however, much of the spectacular forest life has gone.

According to a recent estimate, unless some sort of drastic action is taken very soon, almost all Madagascar's forests will have disappeared within quarter of a century, and with them many species of flora and fauna that are exclusive to this region. If rareties such as many types of screw pines and exotic palms, birds like the serpent eagle, and the island's red-ruffed lemurs are to survive, these forested regions must remain undisturbed.

A gradual change in climate involving a decrease in annual rainfall is partly responsible for the disappearing forests.

But human activity is undeniably mostly to blame. As the local population increased substantially, so trees were felled in favor of farmland, while poachers brazenly took lemurs and other animals from the depths of the island's nature reserves to sell as food and for the wildlife trade.

However, conservationists are determined to revive ancient Madagascan traditions that hold the forests as sacred and worthy of utmost respect. It is an outlook that not only the rest of the continent but the world at large might do well to adopt, too.

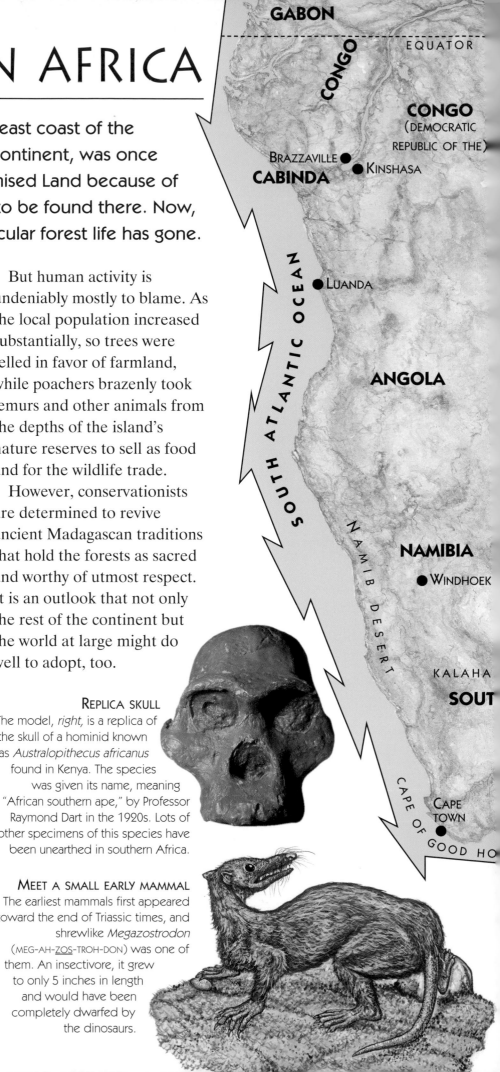

PAINSTAKING WORK
The illustration *below* shows what the hominid whose skull is shown *right* probably looked like. It requires an enormous amount of painstaking work on the part of a paleoanthropologist to make such a reconstruction.

REPLICA SKULL
The model, *right,* is a replica of the skull of a hominid known as *Australopithecus africanus* found in Kenya. The species was given its name, meaning "African southern ape," by Professor Raymond Dart in the 1920s. Lots of other specimens of this species have been unearthed in southern Africa.

MEET A SMALL EARLY MAMMAL
The earliest mammals first appeared toward the end of Triassic times, and shrewlike *Megazostrodon* (MEG-AH-ZOS-TROH-DON) was one of them. An insectivore, it grew to only 5 inches in length and would have been completely dwarfed by the dinosaurs.

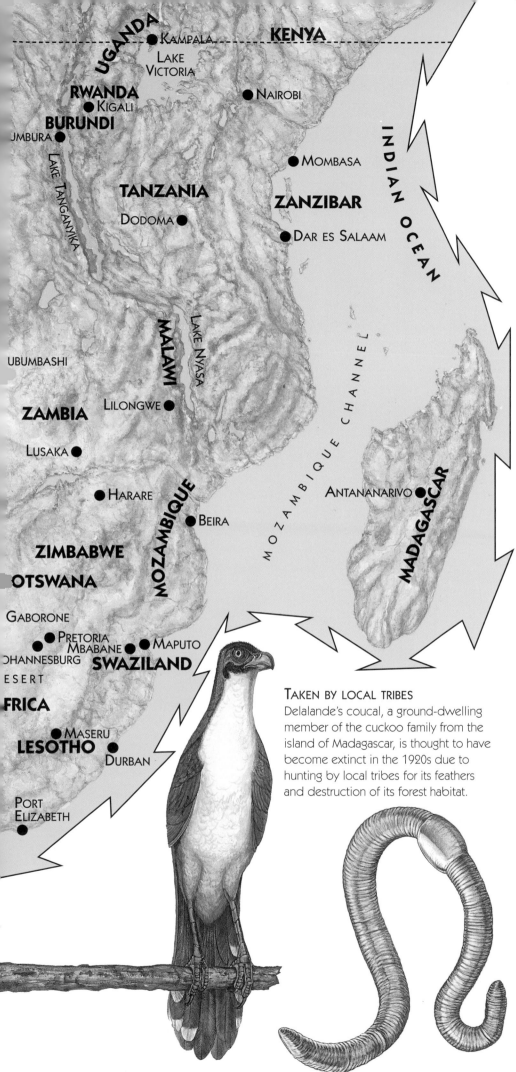

UGANDA
KENYA
● KAMPALA
LAKE VICTORIA
RWANDA
● KIGALI
BURUNDI
JMBURA ●
● NAIROBI

LAKE TANGANYIKA

● MOMBASA

TANZANIA
DODOMA ●
ZANZIBAR
● DAR ES SALAAM

INDIAN OCEAN

UBUMBASHI

MALAWI
LAKE NYASA

ZAMBIA
LILONGWE ●

LUSAKA ●

MOZAMBIQUE CHANNEL

● HARARE
MOZAMBIQUE
● BEIRA

ANTANANARIVO ●
MADAGASCAR

ZIMBABWE
OTSWANA

GABORONE
● ● PRETORIA
MBABANE ● ● MAPUTO
OHANNESBURG SWAZILAND
ESERT
FRICA
● MASERU
LESOTHO
DURBAN

PORT ELIZABETH ●

● Off the map, to the east of Madagascar, are the islands of Mauritius, Rodrigues, and Réunion. It is there that the now-extinct flightless bird the dodo once lived.

● The nearer a country is to the equator, the greater the number of vertebrate, invertebrate, and plant species will be found there. However, scientists are not sure of the reason for this.

A FORMER LINK
Massospondylus (MAS-OH-SPOND-EEL-US) was a quadrupedal sauropod dinosaur from Jurassic times. Its remains have also been found in North America, indicating the two continents were once linked.

TAKEN BY LOCAL TRIBES
Delalande's coucal, a ground-dwelling member of the cuckoo family from the island of Madagascar, is thought to have become extinct in the 1920s due to hunting by local tribes for its feathers and destruction of its forest habitat.

A THREATENED GIANT
One of southern Africa's earthworms, a massive 23 feet in length, is unfortunately fast disappearing due to the desertification of certain regions. Its loss is lamentable because of the importance of such worms in conditioning the soil.

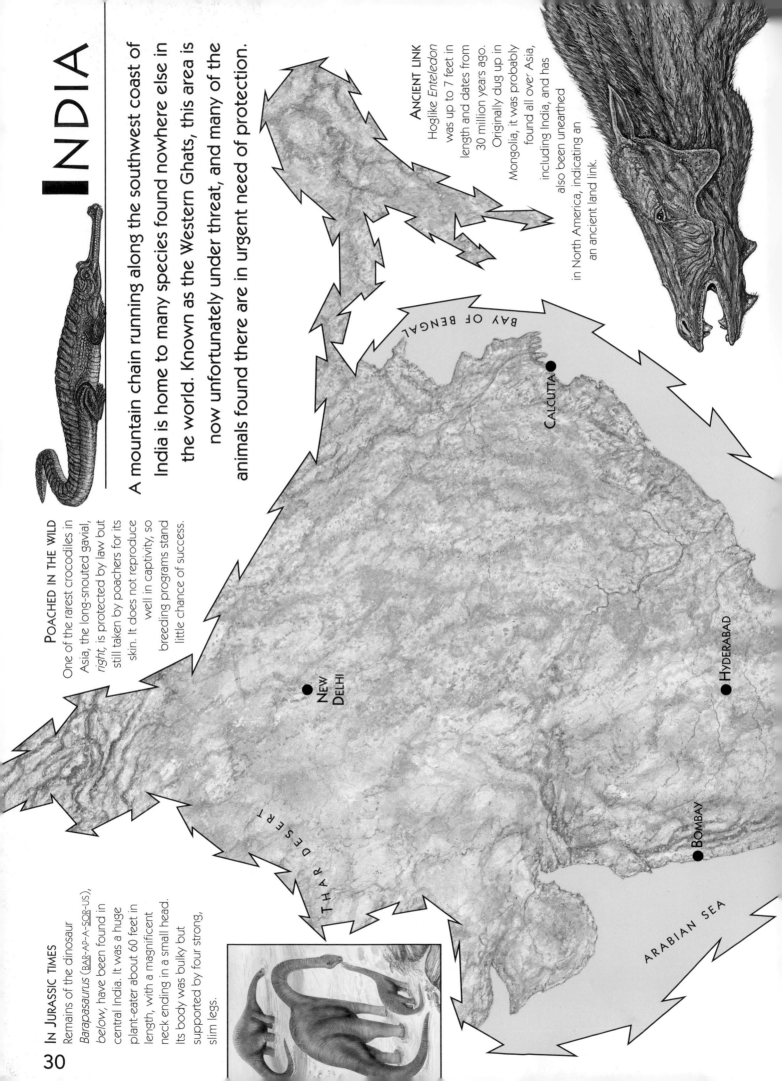

INDIA

A mountain chain running along the southwest coast of India is home to many species found nowhere else in the world. Known as the Western Ghats, this area is now unfortunately under threat, and many of the animals found there are in urgent need of protection.

ANCIENT LINK
Hoglike *Enteledon* was up to 7 feet in length and dates from 30 million years ago. Originally dug up in Mongolia, it was probably found all over Asia, including India, and has also been unearthed in North America, indicating an an ancient land link.

POACHED IN THE WILD
One of the rarest crocodiles in Asia, the long-snouted gavial, *right*, is protected by law but still taken by poachers for its skin. It does not reproduce well in captivity, so breeding programs stand little chance of success.

IN JURASSIC TIMES
Remains of the dinosaur *Barapasaurus* (<u>BAR</u>-AP-A-<u>SOR</u>-US), *below*, have been found in central India. It was a huge plant-eater about 60 feet in length, with a magnificent neck ending in a small head. Its body was bulky but supported by four strong, slim legs.

BAY OF BENGAL

● CALCUTTA

● NEW DELHI

● HYDERABAD

● BOMBAY

THAR DESERT

ARABIAN SEA

Clearly something has to be done before it is too late. But one method of conservation being tried has not proved very successful as yet. In September 2000 a group of scientists from the United States and India began experimenting on a new way of preserving endangered species. They cloned an Asian gaur (an oxlike creature native to India) and implanted the embryo in a cow. It was the first time another species had been used as a surrogate mother. However, Noah, as the baby gaur was named, died from dysentery two days after birth, and no one has yet tried again.

The Western Ghats and the island of Sri Lanka, which were both once linked and part of the same land mass, have long been home to a very rich variety of wildlife and plants. But mining, agriculture, the building of dams, an ever-increasing human population, and the destruction of grasslands and rain forests are now wreaking havoc. Even the area's national park is now feeling the effect as poachers take what they can. At the start of the 20th century there were thought to be over 60,000 square miles of forest in this region. Now, however, the forests have dwindled to under one-twelfth of this.

Fact file

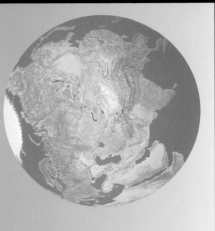

- Forest destruction led to the disappearance of an owl of central India. It is thought to have gone extinct in 1914, when what was possibly the last survivor was shot by an ornithologist as a specimen. In the past even the experts were too hasty in taking examples of a species for the sake of furthering their own name and reputation.

BANGALORE

INDIAN OCEAN

COLOMBO ● SRI LANKA

FADING FAST
Over the last century the Bengal tiger has gone into dramatic decline. Its pelt can fetch a high price, and its bones are also sold as a supposed cure for rheumatism. Those in the wild are seriously endangered.

TIMID BY NATURE
Not seen since 1870, the Himalayan mountain quail was about 1 foot long and did not fly well. It always seems to have been frightened of humans, but no one knows why it disappeared. Few ornithologists ever studied its behavior. The male bird with white head markings is shown in the illustration, *right*.

ONCE RARE BUT RAPID
Jerdon's courser, *left*, went extinct at the beginning of the last century. It had distinctive white bands on its head and seems always to have been rare, which is why very little is known about it except that it flew speedily and avoided open ground.

31

THE MIDDLE EAST

While conservationists from other parts of the planet would like to cooperate closely with those from this region by working with them in the field, unfortunately over recent years it has frequently been the case that such ventures are called to a halt because of political troubles. But dedicated local scientists continue in their attempts to rescue many endangered native species.

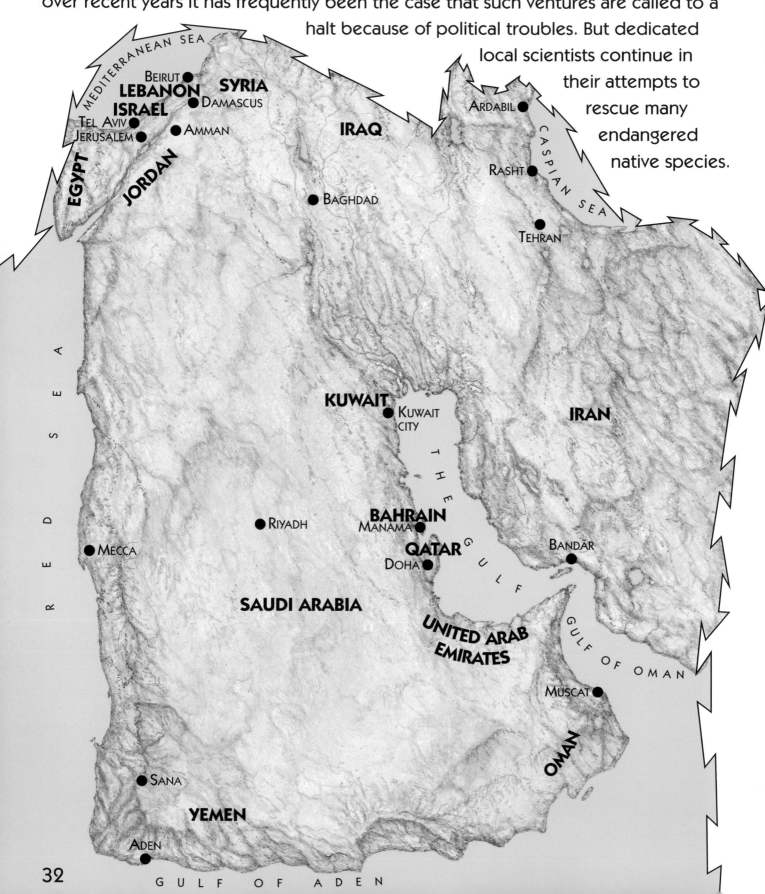

MEDITERRANEAN SEA

BEIRUT
LEBANON   **SYRIA**
ISRAEL   DAMASCUS
TEL AVIV
JERUSALEM   AMMAN
EGYPT   **JORDAN**

IRAQ

BAGHDAD

ARDABIL

CASPIAN SEA

RASHT

TEHRAN

R E D   S E A

KUWAIT   KUWAIT CITY

IRAN

T H E   G U L F

RIYADH   **BAHRAIN**
MANAMA
QATAR   BANDĀR
DOHA

MECCA

SAUDI ARABIA

UNITED ARAB EMIRATES

GULF OF OMAN

MUSCAT

OMAN

SANA

YEMEN

ADEN

GULF OF ADEN

Statistics produced by the World Conservation Union, more commonly known as IUCN after the initials of its original name, show there are currently 13 threatened species in Israel, among them types of bat, gerbil, dugong, and ibex. But in this tiny country about 10% of the land is at least partly environmentally protected. Two sites have also been designated wetlands of international importance because they are home to rare, vulnerable, or endangered plants and animals.

In Jordan, meanwhile, where there are some unique environmental niches, and the flora is diverse even though so much of the country is desert. About 20 species of plants have vanished over the last 100 years. Many more are now rare, some with medicinal uses. There has been a decline in fauna, too; and gazelles, bears, and hyenas are among animals not seen in Jordan for over a century. Many conservation projects are now underway, however, as in other countries of the Middle East.

● Conservationists express concern that although some of the countries of this region are doing a lot to encourage an interest in ecology and endangered species among their populations during times of peace, wars in the Middle East over recent years will inevitably have led to a decline in certain species only found locally, and perhaps the extinction of some of them.

TAKEN FOR MILK AND MEAT
This wild ass from Syria, Arabia, and elsewhere in the region stood only about 3 feet in height but was very swift on its feet. The last known specimen died in 1928. It had always lived mostly in the wild, but some nomads of this area did manage to domesticate and milk it.

ONLY IN OMAN
Currently endangered in Oman but extinct elsewhere in the Arabian Peninsula and land that now forms Israel and Jordan, the Arabian oryx is known for its two slightly curving horns. It was formerly killed for sport and is still poached today in spite of the efforts of Operation Oryx. Bedhouins believe anyone killing an oryx inherits its strength.

OLD BONES
The bones shown *left* are from the skeleton of a male Neanderthal living about 60,000 years ago. They were unearthed by paleoanthropologists in Israel.

DEARLY DEPARTED
Only 55 of the Persian fallow deer shown *below* are thought to exist in the wild following reintroduction into Israel and Iran (once known as Persia.) But reliable statistics are difficult to obtain due to political conflict in that part of the world. Formerly this species, the largest of all the fallow deer, was found in woods in Syria, Jordan, and Iraq, too; but habitat loss and hunting took their toll.

THE FAR EAST

About 30 miles south of China's capital, Beijing, there is a memorial to the past listing all mammals known to have gone extinct since 1900. It is a fitting reminder of the extent to which we all remain responsible for saving today's endangered species and thereby the whole world's natural heritage.

According to a survey made in 1999, there are no more than 20 Siberian tigers in northeast China, and their most important habitat is to be turned into a nature reserve. A hunting ban has also been imposed on the area, and more suitable prey introduced.

CRYING WOLF

The shamanu, *right*, was the smallest known wolf and went extinct in Japan at the beginning of the 20th century. In spite of its size, it had a powerful cry and was greatly feared for some superstitious reason. It was therefore constantly hunted.

FROM THE DEEP

The fossilized plesiosaur skeleton, *left*, dates from Triassic times and was found in China. Its long neck, lengthy tail, small head, and flippers are all clearly visible.

TOKYO

OSAKA

JAPAN

SEA OF JAPAN

PACIFIC OCEAN

NORTH KOREA

P'YŎNGYANG

SOUTH KOREA

SEOUL

YELLOW SEA

EAST CHINA SEA

SHANGHAI

BEIJING

ULAN BATOR

MONGOLIA

CHINA

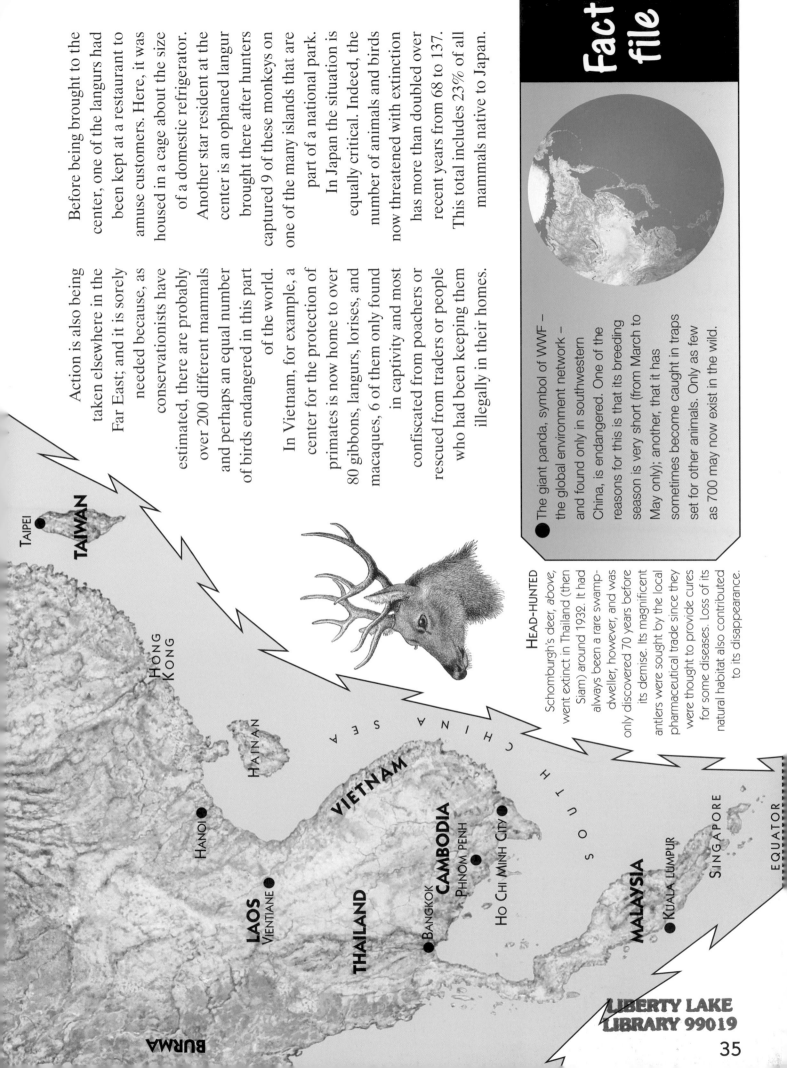

Before being brought to the center, one of the langurs had been kept at a restaurant to amuse customers. Here, it was housed in a cage about the size of a domestic refrigerator. Another star resident at the center is an orphaned langur brought there after hunters captured 9 of these monkeys on one of the many islands that are part of a national park.

In Japan the situation is equally critical. Indeed, the number of animals and birds now threatened with extinction has more than doubled over recent years from 68 to 137. This total includes 23% of all mammals native to Japan.

Action is also being taken elsewhere in the Far East; and it is sorely needed because, as conservationists have estimated, there are probably over 200 different mammals and perhaps an equal number of birds endangered in this part of the world.

In Vietnam, for example, a center for the protection of primates is now home to over 80 gibbons, langurs, lorises, and macaques, 6 of them only found in captivity and most confiscated from poachers or rescued from traders or people who had been keeping them illegally in their homes.

- The giant panda, symbol of WWF – the global environment network – and found only in southwestern China, is endangered. One of the reasons for this is that its breeding season is very short (from March to May only); another, that it has sometimes become caught in traps set for other animals. Only as few as 700 may now exist in the wild.

HEAD-HUNTED
Schomburgh's deer, *above*, went extinct in Thailand (then Siam) around 1932. It had always been a rare swamp-dweller, however, and was only discovered 70 years before its demise. Its magnificent antlers were sought by the local pharmaceutical trade since they were thought to provide cures for some diseases. Loss of its natural habitat also contributed to its disappearance.

TAIWAN
TAIPEI

HONG KONG

HAINAN

SOUTH CHINA SEA

VIETNAM
HANOI

LAOS
VIENTIANE

THAILAND
BANGKOK

CAMBODIA
PHNOM PENH

HO CHI MINH CITY

MALAYSIA
KUALA LUMPUR

SINGAPORE

EQUATOR

BURMA

LIBERTY LAKE
LIBRARY 99019

RUSSIA AND NEIGHBORS

European bison were extinct in the wild by 1924, only a few specimens remaining in zoos around the world after that. A few attempts at reintroduction of the species have since been made with varying degrees of success. Now, however, other promising plans are afoot.

Related to the American buffalo but mainly a forest-dwelling animal, the European bison stands 6.5 feet tall and weighs as much as 10 stocky adult men, while its thick covering of body hair helps it cope with temperatures many degrees below zero. This massive creature was once widely hunted for its flesh and horns, and features in many European cave paintings.

At the beginning of the new millennium 11 captive-bred bison were released from Finnish and German zoos into forests on the Russian-Ukrainian border, where the World Wide Fund for Nature will be watching their progress with interest. The only way to be sure the species stands the best chance of survival is to maintain a good gene pool, so that there is not too much inbreeding among those already in the region. Over a few years the aim is gradually to introduce more of the species until there are about 150. It is hoped that this core population would then grow to approximately one thousand. Poaching must again be guarded against, however.

LOST TIGERS

The last time anyone saw a Caspian tiger was in the 1950s, and it is now presumed extinct, although there are occasional reports of a mysterious large catlike animal in the region of the Caspian Sea. The males of the species *Panthera tigris virgata* were about 9 feet long, and the females, a lot smaller in size. The largest males weighed a hefty 520 pounds.

RUSSIA

ST. PETERSBURG

MOSCOW

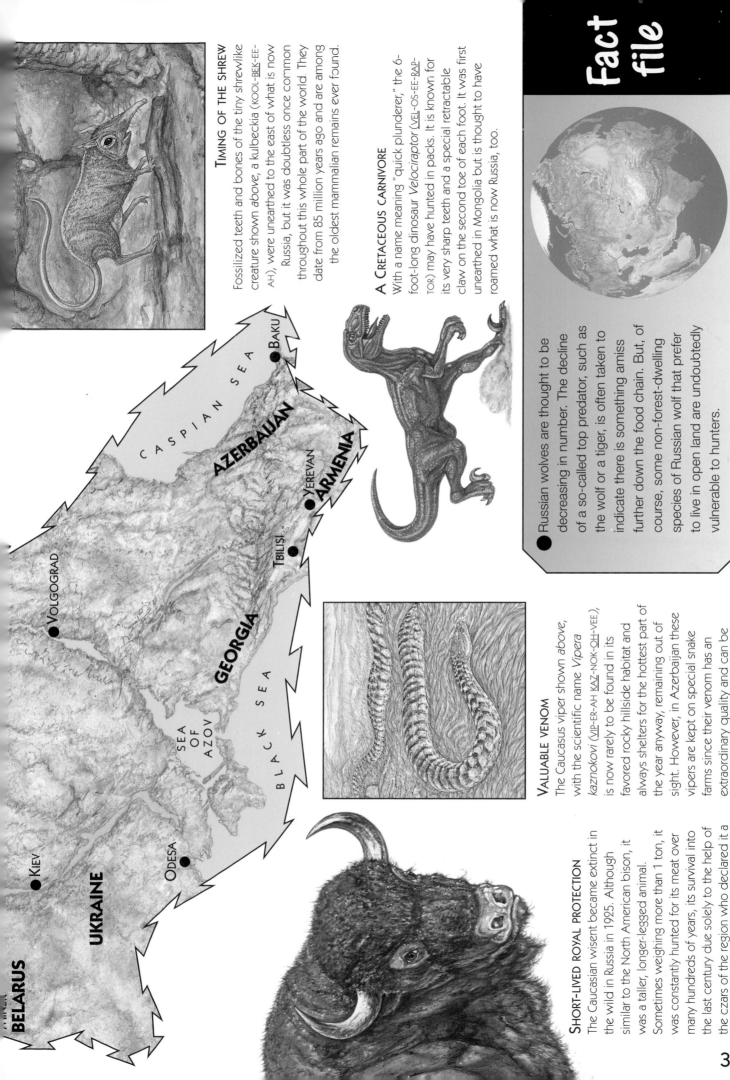

TIMING OF THE SHREW

Fossilized teeth and bones of the tiny shrewlike creature shown *above*, a kulbeckia (KOOL-<u>BEK</u>-EE-AH), were unearthed to the east of what is now Russia, but it was doubtless once common throughout this whole part of the world. They date from 85 million years ago and are among the oldest mammalian remains ever found.

A CRETACEOUS CARNIVORE

With a name meaning "quick plunderer," the 6-foot-long dinosaur *Velociraptor* (<u>VEL</u>-OS-EE-<u>RAP</u>-TOR) may have hunted in packs. It is known for its very sharp teeth and a special retractable claw on the second toe of each foot. It was first unearthed in Mongolia but is thought to have roamed what is now Russia, too.

- Russian wolves are thought to be decreasing in number. The decline of a so-called top predator, such as the wolf or a tiger, is often taken to indicate there is something amiss further down the food chain. But, of course, some non-forest-dwelling species of Russian wolf that prefer to live in open land are undoubtedly vulnerable to hunters.

BAKU

CASPIAN SEA

AZERBAIJAN

YEREVAN • ARMENIA

TBILISI

GEORGIA

VOLGOGRAD

SEA OF AZOV

BLACK SEA

ODESA

KIEV

UKRAINE

BELARUS

VALUABLE VENOM

The Caucasus viper shown *above*, with the scientific name *Vipera kaznokovi* (<u>VIP</u>-ER-AH <u>KAZ</u>-NOK-<u>OH</u>-VEE), is now rarely to be found in its favored rocky hillside habitat and always shelters for the hottest part of the year anyway, remaining out of sight. However, in Azerbaijan these vipers are kept on special snake farms since their venom has an extraordinary quality and can be used to help stop bleeding.

SHORT-LIVED ROYAL PROTECTION

The Caucasian wisent became extinct in the wild in Russia in 1925. Although similar to the North American bison, it was a taller, longer-legged animal. Sometimes weighing more than 1 ton, it was constantly hunted for its meat over many hundreds of years, its survival into the last century due solely to the help of the czars of the region who declared it a protected species.

37

THE BRITISH ISLES

In Great Britain one of the first signs of spring has always been the sound of the cuckoo. However, this seasonal call is now heard far less frequently, reflecting a serious decline in the numbers of this bird, particularly in woodland areas that are fast disappearing. The Woodland Trust – Great Britain's leading woodland conservation organization – has expressed concern about the fate of this species.

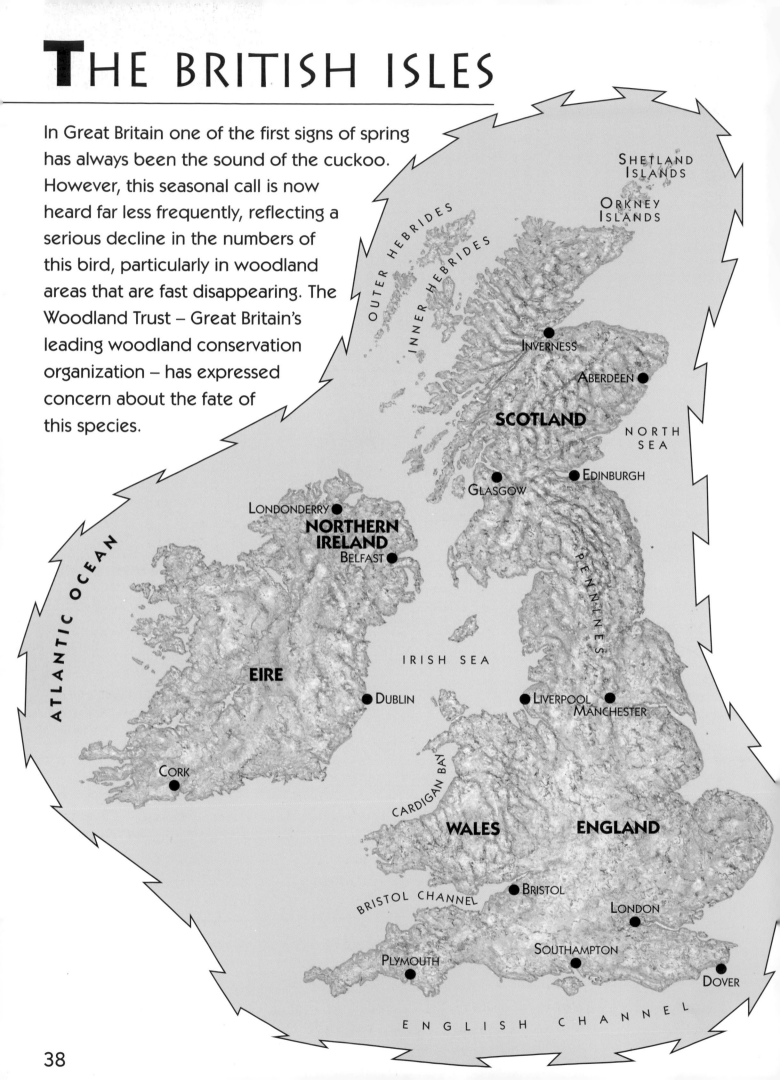

SHETLAND ISLANDS

ORKNEY ISLANDS

OUTER HEBRIDES

INNER HEBRIDES

INVERNESS

ABERDEEN

SCOTLAND

NORTH SEA

GLASGOW

EDINBURGH

LONDONDERRY

NORTHERN IRELAND

BELFAST

PENNINES

ATLANTIC OCEAN

EIRE

IRISH SEA

DUBLIN

LIVERPOOL

MANCHESTER

CORK

CARDIGAN BAY

WALES

ENGLAND

BRISTOL

BRISTOL CHANNEL

LONDON

SOUTHAMPTON

PLYMOUTH

DOVER

ENGLISH CHANNEL

38

MAMMOTH SURPRISE

The workers in the photograph *above* are struggling to remove a covering of protective plaster from a mammoth bone unearthed in southeast England. During the last Ice Age these gigantic animals were to be found throughout Great Britain, and their remains continue to turn up every now and then in some unexpected locations.

CONSERVING A COLORFUL CREATURE

The marsh fritillary butterfly is in severe decline in southwest England, Wales, and Northern Ireland, where its wet meadow habitat has been under threat. Its breeding sites are the subject of an action plan and protected by a European directive, however.

The red squirrel has also declined dramatically over the last 100 years in Great Britain and is hardly ever seen today throughout most of England, Wales, and southern Scotland, due mainly to introduction of a competitor – the gray squirrel from North America – in the 1870s. But disease and habitat destruction have also had considerable impact.

BOGLAND BEAST

The Irish elk became extinct in what is now Northern Ireland and Eire about 10,000 B.C. It stood 10 feet in height and was therefore larger than the moose of North America. It is is more likely to have inhabited boglands than forests because of the tremendous size of its antlers.

A CRETACEOUS FISH-EATER

Fossilized remains found in the stomach cavity of *Baryonyx* (BAR-EE-ON-IKS) led scientists to believe it ate fish. Unearthed in southern England, dating from Cretaceous times, and about 30 feet in length, *Baryonyx's* large thumb claws were possibly used for spearing its prey.

A species recovery program that was set up in 1991 by a body known as English Nature, the British government's official wildlife watchdog, to save just a handful of species from extinction is now concerned with over 600 different forms of flora and fauna. Some of its success stories lend a note of optimism to the situation, however.

Fact file

● When the Large Blue butterfly became extinct in England in 1979, scientists investigating its demise found it was due to dependence of its caterpillar on a particular species of red ant that it parasitized. These ants had gradually vanished from the countryside due to changes in farming methods. Now, however, the Large Blue and the ants have been successfully reintroduced.

IN THE PREHISTORIC SKIES

Discovered in England, *Ornithocheirus* (ORN-EETH-OH-CAYR-US), a Cretaceous pterosaur, had a wingspan of over 8 feet, a short tail, and strong teeth.

A captive breeding strategy for the dormouse, for example, has led to excellent recovery for this species; the lady's slipper orchid, formerly an extreme rarity, is now found at 10 sites; and there are currently over 400 breeding pairs of a type of bird that faced imminent extinction, the red kite. The last specimen of the starfruit plant has even been rescued.

Northern Europe

Throughout recent history Europe has been regarded as one of the most culturally advanced areas of the world, bringing its influences to many other parts of the planet. Yet only over the last few decades has it woken up to the effects of environmental damage.

Paleontologists working in this part of the globe have found lots of exciting fossil evidence for creatures that went extinct in prehistoric times, long before this territory became divided by many borders into all the independent countries existing there today. Some are shown across these two pages. In recent times this region's wildlife has been mainly affected by human action.

Indeed, pollution has become an ever-increasing problem within this highly industrialized zone, where acid rain has been causing damage to forests and lakes over the last 50 years. Thankfully, however, conservation groups in every country of the region are now working actively both to protect particular endangered species and to force industry to reduce harmful emissions.

BURIED AT SEA
This fossil of an extinct crustacean dates from the Cenozoic era and is therefore at least 2 million years old. At that time the sea would have covered much of what is now Germany, but subsequently receded.

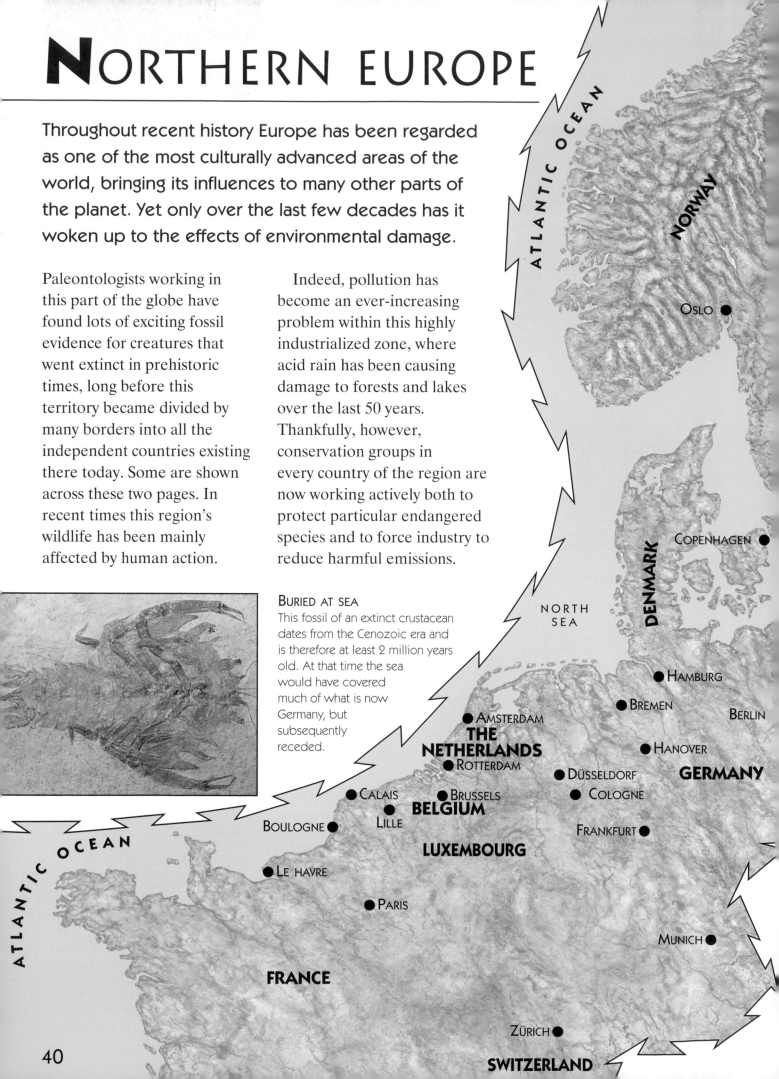

ATLANTIC OCEAN

NORWAY

OSLO ●

DENMARK

COPENHAGEN ●

NORTH SEA

● HAMBURG

● BREMEN

BERLIN

● AMSTERDAM

THE NETHERLANDS

● HANOVER

● Rotterdam

● DÜSSELDORF

GERMANY

● Calais

● Brussels

● COLOGNE

BELGIUM

BOULOGNE ●

LILLE

● FRANKFURT

LUXEMBOURG

● LE HAVRE

● PARIS

ATLANTIC OCEAN

MUNICH ●

FRANCE

ZÜRICH ●

SWITZERLAND

GULF OF BOTHNIA

FINLAND

● HELSINKI

SWEDEN

● STOCKHOLM

● TALLINN

ESTONIA

BALTIC SEA

● RIGA

LATVIA

LITHUANIA

VILNIUS ●

POLAND

WARSAW ●

Fact file

● Members of the Swedish public are encouraged to monitor threatened wild flowers. They are known as Flora Guardians.

● In France there are many national parks and a large number of nature reserves that apply stringent regulations. Marshlands, mountain areas, and moorlands are examples of areas protected in this way.

BONE BONANZA

Two-hundred-million-year-old remains of one of a family of dinosaurs known as plateosaurids (PLAT-EE-OH-SOR-IDS) have been found at more than 50 sites in France, Germany, and Switzerland. As you can see, they could rear up on their hind legs to feed from tall trees.

FROM THE DISTANT PAST

A long-extinct fossil rhinoceros, known by the scientific name *Diaceratherium lemanense* (DEYE-AS-ER-AY-THEER-EE-UM LEM-AN-EN-SAY), is shown in the photograph, *above*, being excavated at a fossil site in France. No species of this creature is found in the wild in Europe today.

FROM JURASSIC GERMANY

With a name meaning "ancient wing," *Archaeopteryx* (ARK-EE-OPT-ER-IKS) was a 3-foot-long, feathered link between dinosaurs and birds. It could not take to the skies but fluttered and had clawed fingers on its wings.

CENTRAL EUROPE

War usually results in human deaths, but it is also totally environmentally unfriendly. During the recent war in the area around Yugoslavia, for example, a number of nature reserves and national parks were subjected to bombing, possibly causing long-term harm to the plant and animal life endemic to the region.

It is not only direct hits that may have harmed some of the wildlife of this region. When certain industrial buildings are targeted during war, for example, toxic chemicals are sometimes released, causing harmful air pollution and possibly spillage into rivers. Fires can prove hazardous to flora and fauna, too.

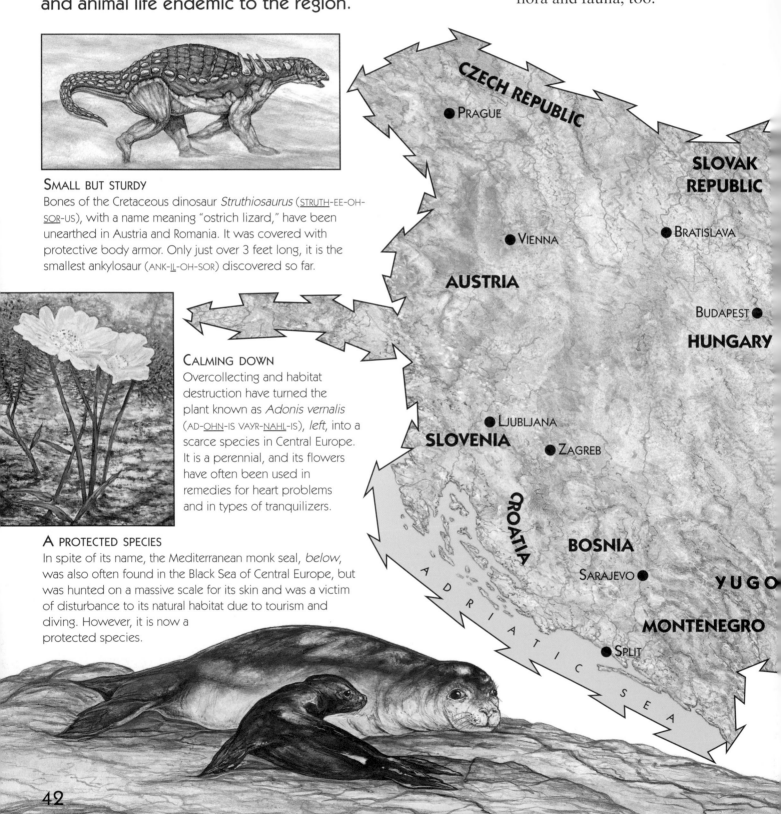

SMALL BUT STURDY
Bones of the Cretaceous dinosaur *Struthiosaurus* (STRUTH-EE-OH-SOR-us), with a name meaning "ostrich lizard," have been unearthed in Austria and Romania. It was covered with protective body armor. Only just over 3 feet long, it is the smallest ankylosaur (ANK-IL-OH-SOR) discovered so far.

CALMING DOWN
Overcollecting and habitat destruction have turned the plant known as *Adonis vernalis* (AD-OHN-IS VAYR-NAHL-IS), *left*, into a scarce species in Central Europe. It is a perennial, and its flowers have often been used in remedies for heart problems and in types of tranquilizers.

A PROTECTED SPECIES
In spite of its name, the Mediterranean monk seal, *below*, was also often found in the Black Sea of Central Europe, but was hunted on a massive scale for its skin and was a victim of disturbance to its natural habitat due to tourism and diving. However, it is now a protected species.

CZECH REPUBLIC

● PRAGUE

SLOVAK REPUBLIC

● BRATISLAVA

● VIENNA

AUSTRIA

BUDAPEST ●

HUNGARY

● LJUBLJANA

SLOVENIA

● ZAGREB

CROATIA

BOSNIA

SARAJEVO ●

YUGO

MONTENEGRO

● SPLIT

A D R I A T I C   S E A

In this part of central Europe, and in other countries of the region, too, however, a lot is now being done to safeguard the local wildlife heritage. The World Society for the Protection of Animals now has disaster relief teams to help save animals caught in war zones or natural catastrophes. They act in peacetimes, too, and in Hungary, for example, have set up a sanctuary for bears, which are a dwindling species in the region. Here, too, conservationists have noticed a growing number of other endangered species, but new national parks are being set up.

Densely forested areas are fortunately still to be found in Romania, the Czech Republic, Slovakia, Bulgaria, and Slovenia, and they remain relatively undisturbed. Nevertheless, if these countries are grouped together, estimates of the numbers of endangered species run into hundreds.

Air pollution, some of it from mining, the poaching of animals for food, urban development, and the picking of rare herbs and other plants have combined to threaten the biodiversity of this area. There will always be a limited amount local legislation can achieve.

Fact file

● Many migrant birds cross vast areas of Central Europe, and it is vital for them, too, that the environment of the region is maintained.

● Some of the world's foremost herbalists come from Central Europe and are very aware of the importance of ensuring certain rare medicinal plants are not placed at further risk through carelessness.

ROMANIA

● BELGRADE

● BUCHAREST

SERBIA
LAVIA

VARNA ●

BULGARIA

● SOFIA

KOSOVO
● SKOPJE

● PLOVDIV

MACEDONIA

B L A C K   S E A

GOING BATS
The bizarre-looking Barbastelle bat, *above*, is currently highly vulnerable in many Central European countries due to destruction of its natural habitat and a reduction in its insect prey.

MISSING FROM EUROPE'S MEADOWS
The bird *right* is a corncrake, now rare due mainly to loss of its natural habitat, the hay meadows of Central Europe. Over the last part of the 20th century, its numbers are thought to have declined by 20-50%.

SOUTHERN EUROPE

One of the greatest problems facing the countries of this area during the last half of the 20th century was severe pollution of the Mediterranean Sea. It was made worse by the fact that these waters have very little outflow, so that effluents accumulated.

At one stage the state of the Mediterranean Sea was so bad that even though tourists still flocked to its shores, it was considered among the most polluted waters of the world.

What was required was a combined effort on the part of all countries bordering the Mediterranean – not only those of southern Europe, of course, but also those of North Africa on the other side of the sea.

This did come about, and conditions gradually improved, although they are still far from ideal. Polluted waters and dirty beaches are not only dangerous to the health of humans, they can also affect the fate of rare marine species, some of which may succomb to extinction.

Sewage has not been the only area of concern. When accidents happen and tankers leak oil, that is bad enough. But when vessels intentionally dump oil into the sea, the effect will be widespread, causing harm to all sorts of sea creatures, some possibly already rare.

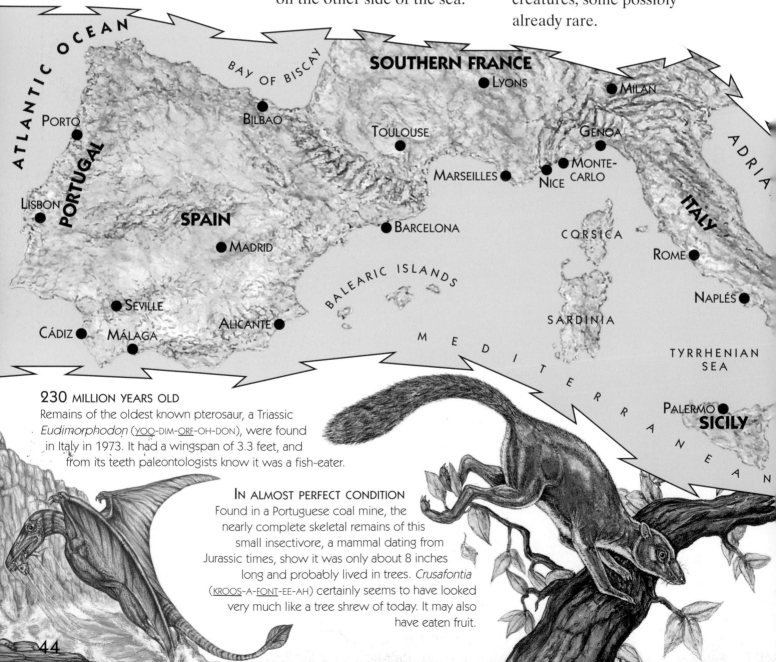

ATLANTIC OCEAN

BAY OF BISCAY

SOUTHERN FRANCE

• LYONS

• MILAN

PORTO •

BILBAO •

TOULOUSE •

GENOA •

ADRIA

LISBON •

PORTUGAL

SPAIN

• BARCELONA

MARSEILLES •

MONTE-CARLO •

NICE

CORSICA

ITALY

• MADRID

ROME •

SEVILLE •

BALEARIC ISLANDS

NAPLÉS •

CÁDIZ •

ALICANTE •

SARDINIA

MÁLAGA •

MEDITERRANEAN

TYRRHENIAN SEA

PALERMO •

SICILY

230 MILLION YEARS OLD
Remains of the oldest known pterosaur, a Triassic *Eudimorphodon* (YOO-DIM-ORF-OH-DON), were found in Italy in 1973. It had a wingspan of 3.3 feet, and from its teeth paleontologists know it was a fish-eater.

IN ALMOST PERFECT CONDITION
Found in a Portuguese coal mine, the nearly complete skeletal remains of this small insectivore, a mammal dating from Jurassic times, show it was only about 8 inches long and probably lived in trees. *Crusafontia* (KROOS-A-FONT-EE-AH) certainly seems to have looked very much like a tree shrew of today. It may also have eaten fruit.

FUTURE PROSPECTS?

Named after the mountain range lying between France and Spain, the Pyrenean ibex, *left*, had a thick coat to help it survive harsh winters. Once common, it went into severe decline, and by 1993 only about 10 remained. The last live specimen, a 13-year-old female, was found dead in January 2000, but zoologists have tissue from an ear in case they can ever clone it.

A PORTUGUESE PLANT-EATER

Spiked thumbs, a toothless beak, and lots of closely packed side teeth were the main characteristics of the 30-foot-long, plant-eating dinosaur known as *Iguanodon* (IG-WAHN-OH-DON,) unearthed in Portugal after first having been discovered in England.

TROUBLE FOR THE TURTLES

The beach nesting sites of the loggerhead turtle, *below,* have been seriously affected by an ever-growing tourist industry along the coasts of Greece and Turkey. A number of conservation measures are being adopted, but the economy of this area depends to a large extent on the attraction of its fine resorts.

Fact file

● Cave lions were once found in southern Europe, and their fossilized remains have been discovered alongside those of prehistoric humans. A man-killer known as the European lion also once roamed what is now Greece, but was wiped out before the start of the second century B.C. Not a single species of lion exists today anywhere in the wild in this region.

LIBERTY LAKE
LIBRARY 99019

FRENCH FOSSIL FIND

Discovered among Miocene rocks in France, and therefore several million years old, the fossilized remains of a stocky marine mammal known as *Potamotherium* (POT-AM-OH-THEER-EE-UM), *below left*, show it was small and probably lived partly in the sea and partly on land. It may have been an ancestor of today's sea lions.

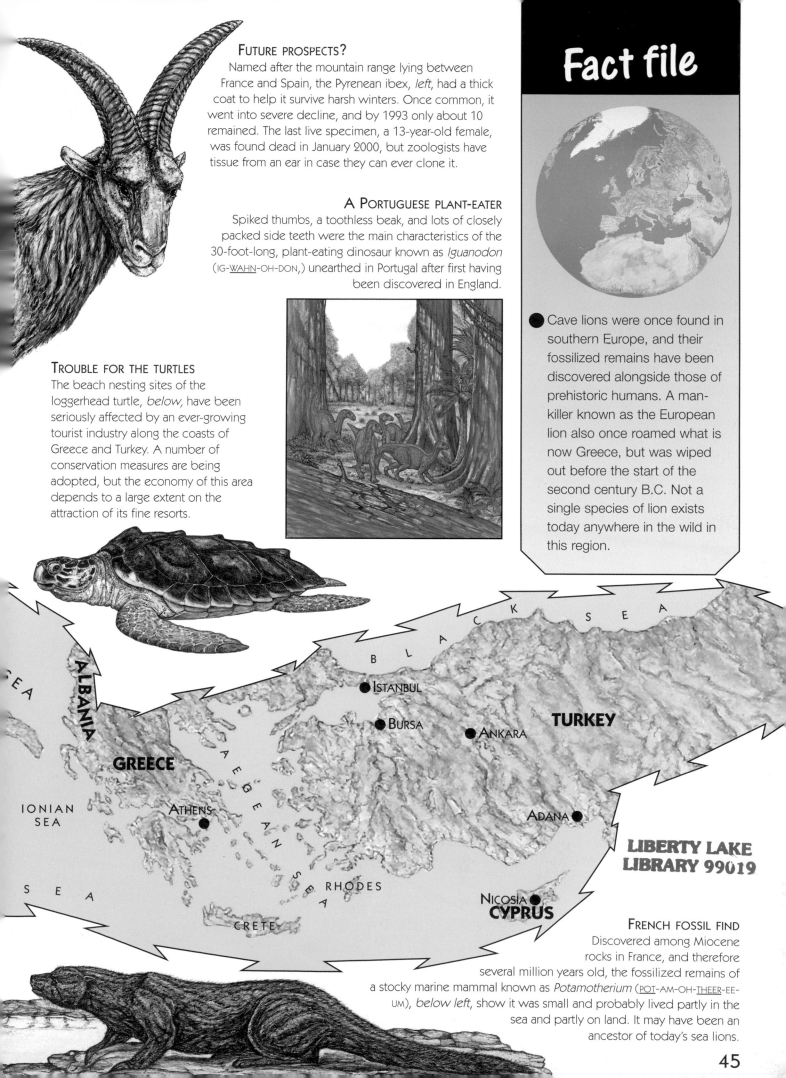

BLACK SEA
ALBANIA
ISTANBUL
BURSA · ANKARA
TURKEY
GREECE
AEGEAN SEA
IONIAN SEA
ATHENS
ADANA ·
SEA
RHODES
NICOSIA ·
CYPRUS
CRETE

GLOSSARY

archipelago
a group of islands

biodiversity
varied types of flora and fauna

biome
a particular sort of
environment such as the
rainforests, desert, or
grasslands

CFCs
an abbreviation for
Chlorofluorocarbons (KLOR-
OH-FLOOR-OH-KAR-BONS),
mostly produced by aerosol
sprays, refrigerators, and air
conditioners, that are harmful
greenhouse gases

conservation
care of flora and fauna

coral reef
the skeletal remains of various
small marine invertebrates

deforestation
the removal of forests

ecologist
not used in another book only...

ecology
the study of plants and animals
in relation to the environment

ecosystem
interaction of living organisms

endemic
particular to a region

fauna
animal life

flora
plants and other vegetation

food chain
a series of organisms connected
by the fact that each forms food
for the next highest in the line

fossil
animal or plant remains
embedded or preserved in
rocks or other material

gene pool
the available genetic material
from a group of organisms,
from which the next
generations will inherit certain
characteristics

habitat
the natural environment of an
animal or plant

hominid
any one of a number of early
humanlike creatures from
which we may possibly be
descended

inbreeding
breeding within a small
population of creatures

invertebrate
a creature without a backbone

mammal
any creature bearing and
suckling live young

marsupial
any animal with a pouch for
carrying its young

megafauna
large animals

Neanderthal
an early hominid

nocturnal
coming out by night

paleontologist
a scientist who studies fossils

predator
an animal that hunts another

prey
the victim of a predator

stratosphere
a layer of the atmosphere
about 7 miles above the surface
of the Earth, where the
temperature is fairly constant

vertebrate
a creature with a backbone

vulnerable
in danger